From Chaos to Clarity

Unlock the Proven Process to Boost Your Win Rates

Angie Wolfe, CP APMP

Ideas at Dawn Marketing Consultants

© 2025 Ideas at Dawn, LLC

All Rights Reserved

Limits of Liability / Disclaimer of Warranty

The authors and publisher of this book and the accompanying materials have used their best efforts in preparing this program. The authors and publisher make no representation or warranties concerning the accuracy, applicability, fitness, or completeness of the contents of this program. They disclaim any warranties(expressed or implied), merchantability, or fitness for any particular purpose. The authors and publisher shall in no event be held liable for any loss or other damages, including but not limited to special, incidental, consequential, or other damages. As always, the advice of a competent legal, tax, accounting, or other professional should be sought. The authors and publisher do not warrant the performance, effectiveness, or applicability of any sites listed in this book. All links are for information purposes only and are not warranted for content, accuracy, or any other implied or explicit purpose.

This book contains material protected under International and Federal Copyright Laws and Treaties. Any unauthorized reprint or use of this material is prohibited.

Image licensed from Sylverarts – stock.adobe.com.

Website:www.ideasatdawn.com

10634Ashwood Court, Highlands Ranch, CO 80129

This book is dedicated to the tireless proposal professionals who balance creativity, strategy, and countless deadlines to help their teams succeed. Your hard work and dedication often go unnoticed, but it is the cornerstone of so many wins.

To my family—Jared, Devin, Henry, Milo, and Chestnut—thank you for your unwavering love and support. Your encouragement has made this journey possible.

And to every mentor, colleague, and friend who has shared their wisdom along the way, this book is a testament to the power of collaboration and perseverance.

Contents

Introduction 1
1. From Ground Zero to Groundbreaker 5
2. Igniting the Vision 9
3. Who Reaps the Rewards? 13
4. Lessons from the Field 17
5. Overcoming Hurdles 21
6. Debunking Myths 25
7. The Winning Formula 29
8. The Power of Teamwork 33
9. Metrics of Impact 37
10. Step-by-Step to Success 41
11. Strategies for Success 47
12. Client-Centric Proposals 51
13. The Art of Persuasion 57
14. Resource Mastery 63
15. Strategic Alignment 69
16. The Cost of Failure 73
17. Tech-Savvy Proposals 79
18. Continuous Growth 85

19.	Success Stories	91
20.	Knowledge is Power	95
21.	The Key Takeaway	101
22.	Getting Started	107
23.	The One Change	113
24.	The Future Landscape	119
25.	Navigating Overwhelm	123
26.	Conclusion	129
About The Author		133
Unlock Proposal Success		137

Introduction

I'm Angie Wolfe, and I'm so excited to have you here! You've taken the first step in transforming how you approach proposals, and I'm thrilled that *From Chaos to Clarity: Unlock the Proven Process to Boost Your Win Rates* is now in your hands. If you're a professional in the thick of proposal development and feeling overwhelmed by the endless demands and deadlines, I want you to know—*you're not alone*. So many of us have been there. But I promise, with the right tools and strategies, that **chaos can turn into clarity**.

For more than 20 years, I've been immersed in proposal development in the Architecture, Engineering, and Construction (AEC) industry. My journey began as an intern at Kiewit's corporate magazine, and it's taken me to managing billion-dollar pursuits and founding Ideas at Dawn Marketing Consultants. At Ideas at Dawn, we're passionate about empowering AEC firms to craft winning proposals confidently and clearly. This experience has allowed me to witness firsthand how a streamlined, client-focused process can transform your proposals and your entire approach to work.

Let's be real—proposal development isn't for the faint of heart. The tight deadlines, complex Requests for Proposals (RFP) requirements, and pressure to outshine the competition can feel too much to handle. I know the late nights, the stressful reviews, and the anxious moments when you wonder if you're doing enough. That's exactly why I wrote this book. From Chaos to Clarity is my way of equipping you with a proven process to reduce stress and help you consistently boost your win rates and elevate your career.

What You'll Gain from This Book

In this book, I've packed two decades of lessons and insights into practical, actionable strategies you can apply immediately. Whether you're new to proposal development or a seasoned pro looking to refine your process, you'll find tools and frameworks designed to make a real difference in your work. Together, we'll tackle the challenges head-on and turn them into opportunities.

Here's a glimpse of what's waiting for you inside:

- **Craft Winning Strategies:** Learn how to tailor your approach to highlight your firm's unique strengths.
- **Create Client-Focused Proposals:** Discover how to connect with evaluators by speaking directly to their needs.
- **Streamline Processes:** Simplify your workflows and eliminate redundancy to save time and energy.
- **Mitigate Risks:** Identify common pitfalls and learn how to avoid costly mistakes in proposal development.
- **Boost Confidence:** Gain the tools and insights to lead your team with clarity and assurance.

I poured my heart into this book because I genuinely care about your success. I've been in your shoes, and I understand the challenges you face. My goal is to help you navigate those challenges with a sense of control and purpose. Each chapter is packed with actionable advice designed to guide you step-by-step toward creating proposals that win.

This Book is a Resource, Not Just a Read

As you dive into this book, remember that it's not just something to read—it's a resource built for you. Use it to map out your strategies, refine your processes, and transform how you approach your work. *Proposal development doesn't have to feel like an uphill battle anymore.* With this guide, you'll have the clarity and confidence to tackle even the most complex pursuits.

And here's the best part—you're not alone on this journey. I'd love to connect with you as you implement these strategies. Follow me on LinkedIn for tips, insights, and community discussions. Whether you're facing a specific challenge or want to stay inspired, I'm here to support you every step of the way.

Let's Do This!

Thank you for trusting me to be part of your journey. Together, we will transform your approach to proposals—from *overwhelming* and *chaotic* to **streamlined** and **empowering**. Open these pages with excitement, take notes, and apply what resonates. Your goals are within reach, and I can't wait to see what you achieve.

Happy reading, and here's to your success!

– Angie Wolfe

NOTES

Chapter 1

From Ground Zero to Groundbreaker

My AEC Journey

When I first stepped into the AEC industry, my path was anything but traditional. Armed with a journalism degree from the University of Kansas, I graduated in December 2002, uncertain about my next move. Traditional broadcasting and print journalism didn't feel right for me. But rather than settle, I saw an opportunity to apply my communication and marketing skills in a different sector—one where storytelling met strategy and innovation.

In January 2003, I moved back to Omaha to live with my sister and her family, ready to explore professional opportunities. That's when I found an internship with Kieways, a magazine published by Kiewit Corporation. At the time, I had no idea how transformative this role would be—not only for my career but for my perspective on how stories shape industries like construction.

The Intersection of Storytelling and Construction

As an intern, my job was to dive into the stories behind Kiewit's construction projects. I interviewed project managers, engineers, and other stakeholders, uncovering narratives about design innovation, overcoming challenges, and safety and quality priorities. These weren't just updates on construction—they were stories that captured the human element behind the projects.

This experience helped me see beyond the plans. It let me connect with the people and ideas that fuel the AEC industry. Writing about these projects taught me how to distill complex technical concepts into compelling stories that resonated with a wide audience—a skill that has proven invaluable in proposal development.

A Crash Course in Proposal Management

The real turning point came from the department structure I worked in. It was a small team. Just me and my manager were responsible for the magazine. Then, I and a few others for the proposal efforts across the U.S. and Canada. It was a dual role that opened my eyes to the critical importance of proposals in the AEC industry.

While most of our proposals were geared toward securing federal contracts, the skills I developed transcended any single sector. I learned how to identify and articulate the unique value propositions that make a bid stand out. Proposals weren't just checklists or formalities—they were strategic tools designed to communicate why our team was the best choice for the job.

This crash course in proposal management taught me how to shape submissions around client needs, ensuring they checked the compliance boxes and told a story that resonated. Those early experiences helped me develop a foundational understanding of the nuances of proposal management and writing—a skill set I've carried with me ever since.

Shaping My Career and Perspective

Looking back, my internship wasn't just a stepping stone; it was a masterclass in storytelling, marketing, and the intricacies of construction. The journalism skills I brought to the table—writing, interviewing, and connecting with an audience—allowed me to bring something fresh to the AEC industry. Over time, I transitioned from being an intern to a more strategic role, contributing to how we approached proposals. I found myself influencing the execution and the direction of our bid strategy, refining my skills to align with the evolving needs of the industry.

Today, I credit much of my success to that grounding in journalism. My ability to tell a story—whether it's about a project, a team, or a solution—has become a critical differentiator in a competitive market. In the AEC industry, the way we present a proposal can mean the difference between securing the job or falling short. Strong narratives that connect with clients on both a technical and emotional level can be transformative.

Lessons for AEC Professionals and Beyond

For those navigating their own paths—whether you're a seasoned proposal professional or new to the AEC industry—remember that your unique background can become your greatest asset. Even if they feel unrelated, the skills you bring can be cultivated into niche expertise that sets you apart.

My journey from intern to industry leader is proof that no matter where you start, there's room to grow, learn, and thrive. Embrace the opportunities to refine your craft, take ownership of your narrative, and focus on the stories you want to tell—because those stories ultimately connect us to the clients, teams, and communities we serve.

Key Takeaways

- **Leverage storytelling skills:** Use narrative techniques to craft compelling proposals that resonate with clients and evaluators.

- **Embrace your unique background:** Highlight how your diverse skills and experiences can add depth and value to your role in AEC marketing.

- **View proposals as strategic tools:** Approach them as powerful, persuasive documents that can secure business and strengthen client relationships.

- **Continuously seek learning opportunities:** Stay proactive in refining your approach and adopting new strategies to remain competitive in the industry.

NOTES

Chapter 2

Igniting the Vision

Why This Book on Proposal Management?

In the AEC industry, proposals are more than just submissions—they are the gateway to opportunity. After years of being immersed in this field, I felt compelled to write this book on proposal management to share my experiences and amplify the collective voices of professionals I've had the privilege to meet. This book is designed to fill the gaps, especially for people who feel uncertain or overwhelmed, whether they're stepping into proposal management or have been navigating its complexities for years.

For many, the path to working on proposals is anything but deliberate—it's accidental. You might find yourself here because your talents align with your firm's needs, but chances are, formal training in proposal development was never part of the equation. This gap can leave even the most capable professionals feeling unprepared and frustrated. This book is also for the seller-doers—the industry experts juggling multiple roles while tackling proposals. My goal is to equip you with proven techniques and frameworks that elevate your proposals and make the process more manageable. Imagine working within a structured process that *simplifies your workload*, *reduces chaos*, and *turns deadlines into achievable milestones*. That's the power of a **systematic approach**.

Breaking Down Barriers and Building Community

Throughout my career, I've had countless conversations with proposal professionals across industries. While their challenges differ, one common thread is their isolation in their roles. This is especially true in the AEC industry, where proposal teams often operate in silos, missing out on opportunities to share knowledge and strategies. This book aims to break down those silos, fostering a sense of community among professionals. By encouraging collaboration and connection, we can create a more cohesive and supportive environment for proposal development.

This isn't just a resource—it's a rallying cry for professionals to come together, exchange ideas, and champion a better way of working. The strategies and insights within these pages are designed to empower you to excel in your role and elevate your entire team. **Proposal management doesn't have to be a lonely endeavor; it can be a shared journey toward success.**

Driving Change and Building Confidence

This book is also a tool to help you advocate for yourself and your ideas within your organization. Proposal management is more than just meeting deadlines; it's about understanding what *makes a proposal stand out*. When you master this craft, you become an invaluable asset to your firm—someone who can influence outcomes and drive growth.

With the knowledge you'll gain here, you'll have the tools to confidently lead proposal efforts, introduce innovative ideas, and position your firm as a frontrunner in a competitive market. The confidence that comes with mastering your role will transform your career and empower you to be a catalyst for change within your organization.

Balancing the Chaos

Let's be honest—proposal management is demanding. Deadlines are relentless, priorities shift, and the workload can feel like a never-ending tide. Balancing professional responsibilities with personal commitments is no small feat, but it is possible. This book offers practical insights into resource allocation, task management, and forecasting to help you stay in control. By embracing these strategies, you'll create a sense of balance in your work, reducing stress while meeting deadlines with precision.

The goal is to help you manage proposals and thrive in the process. With the right tools and mindset, you can navigate even the most challenging projects with confidence and agility.

A Call to Action

This book is designed to inspire you to think differently, work smarter, and achieve more. It's about empowering you to take ownership of your role, improve your processes, and ultimately drive success for yourself and your firm.

As you dive into the chapters ahead, I hope you'll find insights that resonate with your experiences. Each strategy is crafted to help you build better proposals and find clarity, purpose, and confidence in your work. Together, you can **transform how proposals are managed** and pave the way for greater success—*for you, your team, and the industry.*

> ### Key Takeaways
>
> - **Embrace a structured approach:** Simplify proposal development, reduce chaos, and turn deadlines into manageable milestones.
>
> - **Foster collaboration:** Break down silos to build a supportive community of proposal professionals.
>
> - **Advocate for innovation:** Use proven techniques to elevate proposals, drive change, and position your firm as a market leader.
>
> - **Balance workload and responsibilities:** Apply practical strategies to reduce stress, meet deadlines, and thrive in the proposal process.

NOTES

Chapter 3

Who Reaps the Rewards?

Identifying Beneficiaries of Proposal Success

When creating successful proposals, one of the first questions is, *"Who stands to gain the most from implementing a streamlined, structured approach?"* In the AEC industry—and beyond—there are key players whose success hinges on an efficient process. Understanding these stakeholders is the first step toward optimizing your efforts and driving better outcomes for your team and your organization.

Proposal Staff in the AEC Industry

At the heart of any proposal process are the professionals responsible for pulling it all together. For proposal staff in the AEC industry, the challenges are both unique and daunting: meeting complex compliance requirements, juggling intricate technical details, and battling relentless deadlines. Without a clear roadmap, it's easy to feel overwhelmed.

That's where a structured process becomes a game changer. Establishing clarity and consistency reduces stress and lets the proposal team focus on what matters most—crafting persuasive, client-focused content. When a repeatable process is in place, proposal teams can move confidently from draft to final submission *without the chaos* of competing demands slowing them down.

Proposal Staff in Other Industries

While the spotlight in this book is on AEC, the principles discussed extend well beyond this sector. Industries like IT, healthcare, and space also grapple with tight deadlines, complex requirements, and the need to differentiate. For professionals in these fields, adapting the frameworks outlined here can provide the clarity and efficiency needed to navigate their unique challenges.

Whether it's incorporating kick-off meetings, scheduled reviews, or streamlined templates, these strategies can help ensure consistency and effective collaboration—no matter the industry.

The result?

Higher-quality submissions that resonate with evaluators and maximize the team's potential.

Managers of Proposal Teams

Managers overseeing proposal efforts have one of the toughest jobs. They're tasked with balancing workloads, maintaining team morale, and ensuring every submission is top-notch—all while meeting demanding deadlines. A structured proposal process acts as their secret weapon.

By providing clear benchmarks and timelines, managers can better guide their teams, identify bottlenecks, and foster collaboration. This approach helps *reduce burnout* and *creates an environment where teams can thrive*. When managers embrace these practices, the entire team benefits from a healthier, more productive workflow.

Seller-Doers and Technical Staff

Seller-doers—engineers, architects, and project managers who split their time between client-facing roles and technical contributions—are another critical group. Many lack training in proposal development, which can make the process intimidating. However, integrating these professionals into a structured framework helps demystify their role.

By equipping seller-doers with clear tools, templates, and guidelines, you empower them to contribute effectively. This involvement improves the quality of proposals and strengthens collaboration across teams, turning what might have felt like a burden into a manageable, even rewarding, experience.

Small vs. Large Firms: Tailored Approaches

Firm size plays a significant role in how these processes are implemented. For smaller firms, simplicity is key. A lean, essential approach—such as emphasizing daily updates and disciplined reviews—can help a solo proposal manager handle submissions without feeling overwhelmed.

For larger firms, scalability is the name of the game. A comprehensive framework that incorporates best practices across departments makes sure even with teams of 100 or more, the process remains efficient. In time-sensitive situations, implementing minimum practices, such as kick-off meetings and periodic reviews, can make a meaningful difference.

Real-World Success Stories

The power of these strategies is best seen through real-world examples. Take James W. Fowler: by adopting a systematic proposal approach, even team members with minimal experience made valuable contributions, and the firm saw measurable improvement in their results.

Similarly, Ideas at Dawn, working with Kraemer North America, highlighted the importance of strategy and collaboration. Kraemer's adoption of a structured process with extreme input from seller-doers helped secure a 90% success rate on key pursuits, showing how powerful these frameworks can be when applied effectively.

Collaboration Is Key

The benefits of a structured proposal process are clear. Whether you're a proposal professional in AEC or another industry, a manager overseeing submissions, or a seller-doer trying to balance technical work with proposal contributions, these strategies are designed with you in mind. **A streamlined approach fosters collaboration, reduces stress, and leads to more successful proposals.**

As you implement these practices, remember that consistency is the foundation of success. By embracing clarity and structure, you improve the quality of your submissions and create a more cohesive, productive environment for your team.

The results?

Happier teams, better proposals, and more wins.

Key Takeaways

- **Establish a clear process:** Provide structure to improve proposal quality and focus.

- **Support project managers:** Use frameworks to balance workloads and assess team performance.

- **Engage seller-doers:** Equip technical staff with tools and templates for meaningful contributions.

- **Adapt to firm size:** Tailor strategies for both small and large firms to optimize collaboration and outcomes.

NOTES

Chapter 4

Lessons from the Field

Experiences that Shaped My Proposal Strategy

Proposal development plays an important role in winning work in the AEC industry. With over two decades of experience, I've seen firsthand how this process has evolved—pushing professionals to adapt in ways that were unimaginable years ago. What was once a straightforward response to Requests for Qualifications (RFQs) and Requests for Proposals (RFPs) has grown into a dynamic, strategy-driven process essential for winning work in an increasingly competitive industry.

From unstructured beginnings to putting serious strategies into practice, I've observed that the strongest proposals thrive not on effort alone but on meticulous planning, consistency, and collaboration. In this chapter, we'll explore how structured processes have reshaped the way we approach proposal development and why they're more important than ever in today's fast-paced environment.

The Necessity of Structure in Proposal Development

One of the most valuable lessons I've learned is that structure is the foundation of successful proposal development. A well-defined process brings clarity and focus, even when deadlines are tight or requirements are complex. Establishing core practices like kick-off meetings, color reviews, and compliance checks transforms what could be chaotic projects into streamlined efforts where everyone knows their role.

For example, the Ideas at Dawn team worked with a firm that relied only on the proposal team to respond to RFPs. While their passion was admirable, their lack of strategy led to inconsistent results. By guiding them toward implementing a repeatable process—including defining win themes and holding regular status meetings—they saw a measurable improvement in their proposals' quality and win rates. It's proof that effort alone isn't enough; **structure amplifies success**.

Adapting to Industry Changes

The AEC industry has changed dramatically in the last 20 years. When I started, firms might produce a handful of proposals each year. Now, it's common to manage multiple submissions in a single month. With increased competition, shorter timelines, and reduced page counts, the stakes have never been higher.

Newer delivery methods like progressive design-build (PDB) and construction manager/general contractor (CM/GC) add further complexity, requiring proposals to communicate key differentiators clearly and concisely. In this crowded marketplace, crafting a compelling narrative tailored to the client's needs is no longer optional—it's essential. Adapting to these shifts means emphasizing collaboration, clarity, and client focus to ensure your proposal stands out.

Overcoming Resistance and Educating Internal Stakeholders

Not everyone immediately sees the value of a structured proposal process. I've worked with clients who want exceptional outcomes without investing time in preparation. This disconnect is common across firms of all sizes, but overcoming it requires open communication and education.

When I encounter resistance, I focus on helping clients understand the value of preparation. Structured processes aren't a burden—they're the foundation for achieving results. By highlighting success stories and showing how a thoughtful approach reduces stress and improves outcomes, I've helped even the most skeptical teams embrace the benefits of planning and collaboration.

Building a Flexible Yet Robust Proposal Process

The most successful proposal processes balance adaptability and consistency. Over the years, I've honed a framework that focuses on efficiency, clarity, and alignment with client goals. Whether it's a small firm with limited resources or a large organization tackling dozens of submissions, the same principles apply: **start with the basics, build a strong foundation, and refine as you go**.

For example, instituting a simple kick-off meeting or setting realistic planning milestones can revolutionize how a team handles proposals. Even small changes, like introducing scheduled reviews or leveraging templates, can have an impact on efficiency and outcomes. These tools prepare teams to face challenges confidently and deliver compelling submissions, no matter the circumstances.

Lessons Learned Over Two Decades

The lessons I've learned in my two-plus-decade journey in the AEC industry have shaped my approach to proposal development. Structured processes, strategic foresight, and adaptability aren't just abstract ideas —they're the building blocks of success. Whether you're leading a team or crafting a submission solo, weaving these elements into your work will elevate your proposals and increase your firm's chances of success.

By embracing these practices, you can transform your proposals and how your team collaborates and operates, creating a culture of clarity, consistency, and achievement.

Key Takeaways

- **Structure drives success:** Establishing clear processes like kick-off meetings and compliance checks fosters efficiency and improves outcomes.

- **Adapt to industry changes:** Shorter timelines and increasing competition require strategic and client-focused proposals.

- **Educate and align internal stakeholders:** Communicate the value of preparation to overcome resistance and build support for structured processes.

- **Tailor processes to your needs:** Whether you're in a small firm or a large one, scalable frameworks ensure success at any level.

- **Invest in continuous improvement:** Simple changes like kick-off meetings or scheduled reviews can revolutionize your team's proposal approach.

NOTES

Chapter 5

Overcoming Hurdles

Key Challenges in Proposal Development

Proposal development is not merely an administrative task; it is essential for securing new business and establishing trust with clients. Despite its critical importance, many professionals encounter obstacles that can hinder even the most well-intentioned efforts. Whether you belong to a small firm's lean team or a larger organization's comprehensive department, these challenges are universal. This chapter explores these difficulties and offers practical, actionable strategies to overcome them confidently.

The Pressure of Compressed Timelines

Tight deadlines are one of the most daunting challenges in proposal development. The need to turn around a polished, compelling submission in record time often leads teams to sacrifice important steps. Skipping compliance checks, rushing content revisions, or neglecting collaboration can leave your proposal incomplete.

Think of it like trying to cook a gourmet meal in minutes—you'll inevitably skip steps that make the dish exceptional. To combat this, effective **time management** is key. Break the proposal process into defined phases, assigning specific periods for strategy development, drafting, reviews, and compliance checks. This approach makes sure every critical element gets the attention it deserves, avoiding the chaos of last-minute scrambles.

The Quest for Technical Detail

A lack of project-specific insights can leave your proposal generic and uninspiring. Much like submitting a vague resume for a dream job, proposals that fail to highlight your understanding of the client's needs rarely make the shortlist. Tailoring proposals begins with research—both on the client and the project.

Invest time upfront to gather information that will let you craft a narrative that meets requirements and shows how your expertise uniquely addresses the client's challenges. Highlight your differentiators and align your firm's expertise with the client's vision to stand out from the competition.

Collaborating with Subject Matter Experts

Subject matter experts (SMEs) are a proposal's secret weapon. Their insights bring technical depth and credibility to submissions, but engaging with them can often feel like herding cats. SMEs are busy professionals, and their unavailability can leave proposal teams scrambling to fill the gap with incomplete or overly technical content.

The solution?

Structure your interactions with SMEs to maximize efficiency. Schedule regular, focused check-ins and prepare detailed questions in advance. By respecting their time and targeting specific information, you can extract insights to craft winning proposals while reducing disruptions to their workflow.

Balancing Multi-Disciplinary Expertise

Proposal professionals often wear many hats—writer, editor, designer, and project manager—all within the same project. This juggling act can lead to burnout and compromise the quality of the final product. The key is not to do everything but to leverage tools and templates that streamline repetitive tasks.

For example, **pre-built templates** for resumes, project descriptions, and compliance matrixes can save hours. Embedding these best practices into your process makes sure every submission meets a consistent standard without adding unnecessary stress to your team.

Managing Competing Resources and Responsibilities

Overlapping deadlines are the reality in proposals, especially with the prevalence of best-value procurement methods. Proposal staff are often tasked with juggling multiple submissions while still meeting high standards of quality and compliance. The strain of competing responsibilities can pull teams in different directions, risking errors and missed opportunities.

A **structured approach** helps teams focus effectively. Schedule time for editing and compliance checks as *immovable* milestones in the proposal timeline. Treat these steps as non-negotiable to ensure critical elements remain intact, even when resources are stretched thin.

Tailoring Strategies by Project Type

Proposal challenges differ significantly depending on the size and scope of the project. Small projects often come with limited resources, pushing proposal teams to wear multiple hats and simplify their responses due to page limitations. Larger projects demand detailed narratives, intricate schedules, and greater stakeholder coordination.

Adaptability is the key to success here. For smaller projects, focus on essential elements like compliance and clear messaging. For larger pursuits, dedicate more time to technical details, visuals, and collaboration to meet complex client requirements effectively.

Navigating Different Delivery Models

With delivery models such as design-build and progressive design-build gaining traction, proposal teams face new challenges. These models require **close integration** between technical and proposal teams, making collaboration and customization critical. Understanding the unique needs of each delivery model and tailoring your approach to align with the client's evaluation criteria can set your proposal apart.

Shared Challenges, Collective Solutions

From compressed timelines to the complexities of alternative delivery models, the challenges of proposal development are numerous but not insurmountable. The key lies in adopting strategies that foster collaboration, encourage customization, and focus on structured workflows. By recognizing that these challenges are universal, you can leverage shared solutions to streamline your efforts and produce high-quality proposals that stand out.

The journey to overcoming these hurdles starts with a **commitment to proactive planning**, **team alignment**, and **continuous improvement**. With these strategies, proposal professionals can turn obstacles into opportunities, meeting even the tightest deadlines with confidence and precision.

Key Takeaways

- **Time Management is Critical:** Allocate specific periods for strategy, drafting, and compliance checks to prevent last-minute chaos.

- **Invest in Research:** Tailored proposals require deep client and project insights to craft compelling, customized narratives.

- **Engage SMEs Strategically:** Regular, focused check-ins ensure their expertise is integrated without overwhelming their schedules.

- **Streamline with Tools and Templates:** Simplify repetitive tasks to maintain quality and reduce stress.

- **Adapt to Project and Delivery Models:** Tailor strategies to align with project size, complexity, and unique evaluation criteria.

NOTES

Chapter 6

Debunking Myths

Common Misconceptions in Proposal Development

Proposal development is the gateway to business growth and success. Yet, persistent myths and misconceptions can derail even the most experienced teams. These oversimplified beliefs often lead to mistakes that compromise quality and reduce the likelihood of winning contracts. In this chapter, we'll examine three common misconceptions in proposal development, uncover their implications, and offer strategies to help your team avoid these pitfalls.

Misconception 1: The Process Is Universal

A common myth is that a single proposal process can apply to all projects without adjustment. While consistency is important, each proposal is as unique as the clients it's designed to serve. Think of it like a chef crafting a dish for discerning guests. The recipe may be a guide, but the chef must adapt to available ingredients and the guests' preferences. Similarly, every proposal requires personalization to resonate with its intended audience.

Reusing boilerplate content without customization risks creating submissions that feel generic and impersonal. Such proposals fail to align with client values and priorities, jeopardizing your chances of success. Customizing each proposal to the client's needs, project specifications, and evaluation criteria makes sure your message feels relevant and tailored—qualities that evaluators appreciate and reward.

Misconception 2: The Proposal Team Can Fly Solo

Another myth is that the proposal team can deliver winning submissions without technical input from SMEs. Imagine assembling an intricate piece of furniture without consulting the manual or designer. You might end up with something that looks passable but lacks stability or usability. In proposal development, SMEs provide the technical knowledge and insights to create compelling, credible, and compliant content.

Without SME collaboration, proposals can lack the technical depth needed to differentiate your firm. This oversight leads to shallow narratives, compliance errors, and a failure to show the qualifications evaluators are looking for. Building a culture of collaboration, where SMEs are integrated into the proposal process early and consistently, makes sure your submissions are both accurate and impactful.

Misconception 3: Small Proposals Don't Need a Process

Smaller proposals often fall victim to the misconception that they don't require a structured process. This belief can lead to rushed submissions filled with errors. Just as a small dessert still demands precision in its preparation, even small proposals benefit from diligence and attention to detail.

Skipping steps like compliance checks or collaborative reviews in smaller pursuits increases the risk of disqualification or missed opportunities. A streamlined yet structured process helps maintain quality and consistency across all submissions, no matter their size. By defining minimum steps—like holding a kick-off meeting, conducting a compliance check, and scheduling a final review—you can ensure quality without overburdening your team.

The Implications of These Misconceptions

Believing these myths can have significant repercussions on your proposals. Submissions that reuse boilerplate content often miss the mark, fail to meet evaluation criteria or resonate with clients. Lack of SME involvement can result in superficial technical content that doesn't address project challenges effectively. Neglecting a structured process for smaller proposals can lead to inconsistencies and errors, undermining your credibility.

These issues don't just affect the immediate proposal—they can affect future opportunities by damaging your firm's reputation. A poorly executed submission sends the message that your team isn't detail-oriented or prepared, reducing your competitive edge.

Educating Your Team on Proposal Development

To overcome these misconceptions, educating your team on the value of a structured, collaborative process is critical. Start by defining the minimum steps required for every pursuit, despite the size. This can include:

- A kick-off meeting to align strategy and roles.
- Compliance checks at key milestones.
- Scheduled reviews to refine messaging and address potential issues.

By focusing on these steps, you create a baseline for quality and consistency.

Fostering SME Collaboration

SMEs are key to your proposal process. To engage them effectively, host workshops or training sessions that show the impact of their contributions. Sharing case studies of successful proposals that leveraged SME input can motivate participation and help them see the value of their involvement.

Prepare targeted questions and agendas for SME meetings to ensure their time is used efficiently. This approach fosters a sense of partnership, helping SMEs feel more connected to the proposal's success.

Streamlining Processes for All Proposal Sizes

For small proposals, focus on a simple yet effective framework. Give your team tools like templates, checklists, and responsibility matrices to make the process manageable. For larger pursuits, emphasize collaborative reviews, detailed compliance checks, and comprehensive schedules. Despite the project size, adherence to a structured process ensures that every submission meets quality standards and client expectations.

Building a Culture of Quality

The challenges of proposal development are universal, but they can be addressed by debunking these misconceptions. By focusing on customization, collaboration, and structure, your team can produce high-quality submissions that stand out. Investing time in educating your team, fostering SME engagement, and streamlining processes is an *investment* in your firm's **success**.

Remember: the quality of your proposals reflects your organization's professionalism, credibility, and commitment. A **strong, tailored process** isn't just about winning today's projects—it's about *setting your firm apart for the future*.

Key Takeaways

- **Tailor Every Proposal:** Avoid relying on boilerplate content; customize each proposal to align with client goals and project specifics.

- **Engage SMEs Early:** Incorporate technical knowledge to enrich content and ensure compliance with evaluation criteria.

- **Structured Processes for All Sizes:** Maintain consistency by implementing a streamlined process for small proposals and a comprehensive framework for larger ones.

- **Educate and Empower Teams:** Provide training, tools, and resources to ensure your team understands the value of collaboration and preparation.

- **Foster a Culture of Quality:** Prioritize processes that uphold high standards and reflect your firm's commitment to excellence.

Chapter 7

The Winning Formula

Outlining a Proven Proposal Process

Your proposal can make or break your chances of winning a project. Whether you're a seasoned proposal professional, a manager, or a seller-doer just stepping into the role, the process can feel overwhelming. But here's the good news: success doesn't have to be complicated. With a straightforward six-step process, you can elevate the quality of your proposals while streamlining your efforts to work smarter, not harder.

This chapter is your guide to mastering a proven framework designed to help you and your team create competitive, compelling proposals that win business.

Step 1: Strategy & Pre-Work

Every winning proposal starts with a solid strategy. Before you put pen to paper (or fingers to keyboard), take the time to deeply understand your client. This is where you define your win strategy: pinpoint the client's goals, challenges, and vision of success. Dive into research about the decision-makers and stakeholders—this will help you uncover valuable insights to shape your narrative.

Win themes are the foundation of your strategy. These are the narratives that highlight your team's unique strengths and capabilities. Align these themes with your client's priorities so everyone involved in the proposal process is speaking the same language. This step ensures your proposal is cohesive, client-focused, and persuasive.

Step 2: Kick-Off Meeting

Think of the kick-off meeting as your launchpad. This meeting sets the tone and direction for the entire proposal process. Use this time to align your team around the win strategy and provide clarity on their roles and deadlines. Share essential tools like your compliance matrix and the initial proposal outline, ensuring everyone understands their responsibilities and deliverables.

By fostering a collaborative environment, you reduce the risk of miscommunication and inefficiencies. Encourage open dialogue about potential challenges, and make sure everyone leaves the meeting clear on the plan ahead.

Step 3: Management & Communication

Strong management and consistent communication are the glue that holds the proposal process together. Incorporate daily check-ins, like "Play-of-the-Day" meetings, to keep the team aligned and on track. These short, focused updates ensure accountability, provide a forum for addressing roadblocks, and maintain momentum.

Project management tools can be invaluable here, offering real-time visibility into progress and deadlines. Equip your team with the right tools and ensure everyone is comfortable using them. Clear, consistent communication throughout the process eliminates silos and keeps everyone working toward the same goal.

Step 4: Content Development

This is where the magic happens—your proposal takes shape. Begin with detailed outlines for each section, ensuring they align with the RFP requirements and your win themes. Tailor your content to address the specific client and project. Generic templates might save time, but customized content that speaks directly to the client's needs is what sets your proposal apart.

Engage SMEs early to add technical depth and credibility. Use visuals, case studies, and relevant metrics to reinforce your narrative. By focusing on quality content from the start, you set the stage for a proposal that stands out from the competition.

Step 5: Reviews

A structured review process is essential for creating high-quality proposals. Break it into distinct phases:

- **Pink Team Review:** Focuses on initial content development.
- **Red Team Review:** Ensures alignment with strategy and client priorities.
- **Gold Team Review:** Polishes the final draft for submission.

Involve fresh eyes—team members who didn't draft the sections being reviewed—to catch errors and provide fair feedback. Centralize comments and revisions to streamline the process and avoid duplication of effort using a tool like Adobe Share.

Step 6: Submission, Close-Out, and Debrief

The final step is about execution and reflection. Before hitting "submit," conduct thorough quality checks to ensure the proposal meets all compliance and formatting requirements. Test submission platforms ahead of time to avoid last-minute technical issues.

After submission, gather your team for a debrief. This is your opportunity to celebrate successes, discuss lessons learned, and find ways to improve. A strong debrief process boosts morale and lays the groundwork for continuous improvement in future proposals.

Adapting the Process for Different Teams

One of the greatest strengths of this six-step process is its adaptability. For smaller teams, streamline efforts by focusing on essential steps like kick-off meetings, formal reviews, and compliance checks. Larger teams can assign section leads to maintain efficiency. In quick-turnaround situations, use pre-approved templates to save time without sacrificing quality. For virtual or hybrid teams, leverage collaboration tools to keep everyone connected in real time.

The Power of a Proven Process

A structured proposal process ensures consistency, quality, and compliance across all submissions, despite size or complexity. By fostering collaboration among team members and SMEs, you create accurate, compelling, and client-focused proposals. Regular debriefs allow for continuous improvement, increasing efficiency and win rates.

This six-step process is more than a checklist—it's a mindset. When you commit to following these steps, you're improving your proposals and transforming how your team works. A streamlined, structured approach leads to better proposals, happier teams, and more wins.

Key Takeaways

- **Follow a Proven Process:** The six-step framework ensures alignment, quality, and compliance in all proposals.

- **Tailor Your Approach:** Customize your content and win strategies to address each client's unique needs.

- **Collaboration Is Key:** Engage SMEs and maintain open communication to strengthen technical accuracy and team alignment.

- **Learn and Improve:** Post-submission debriefs provide valuable insights to refine processes and increase win rates.

- **Adaptability Matters:** Flex the process to suit team size, project complexity, and timeline constraints.

Chapter 8

The Power of Teamwork

Enhancing Collaboration in Proposal Development

During proposal development, the value of teamwork cannot be overstated. Developing a proposal without collaboration is like building a sturdy bridge with only half the materials—it won't hold up. Without effective teamwork, proposals end up incomplete, missing the depth, precision, and strategic focus necessary to secure a win in competitive markets.

Collaboration brings together a diverse group of contributors—SMEs, proposal manager, coordinators, writers, graphic designers, and management—each playing a critical role. Together, their knowledge transforms a proposal from a collection of generic information into a cohesive, client-focused document that hits the mark. In this chapter, we'll explore the central role of collaboration in proposal development and provide actionable strategies for building stronger teamwork.

Key Components of Collaboration

1. Collaboration with SMEs: A Non-Negotiable Step

SMEs are the cornerstone of successful proposals. Their deep technical knowledge and project-specific insights give proposals the credibility and precision evaluators demand. Without their input, proposals risk falling flat—becoming vague, uninspired, and ultimately uncompetitive.

The key to engaging SMEs effectively is preparation. Schedule structured interviews and develop focused questions tied directly to the RFP requirements. A well-prepared approach respects their time, builds trust, and increases the chances of gathering the impactful insights your proposal needs.

2. Daily Momentum: The Power of "Play-of-the-Day" Meetings

Quick, focused check-ins—often called "Play-of-the-Day" meetings—are essential for maintaining momentum and accountability. These short meetings keep the team aligned, address obstacles, and ensure progress on key sections of the proposal. By keeping the agenda streamlined and purposeful, these daily or weekly sessions keep everyone informed and engaged without bogging down their schedules.

3. Graphics: Strategic Tools, Not Just Eye Candy

Graphic designers aren't just enhancing the aesthetic appeal of proposals—they're integral to the storytelling process. Visuals clarify complex ideas and reinforce key messages. Involving designers early in the process ensures graphics align with your win themes and complement the narrative. Waiting until the eleventh hour only undermines the quality and impact of your proposal.

Collaborative Techniques That Drive Success

- **Proactive SME Engagement:** Build rapport, set clear expectations, and listen actively. Show SMEs their input is valued by coming prepared with thoughtful questions that align with project goals.
- **Collaborative Tools:** Platforms like Microsoft Teams or Google Workspace enable real-time editing, centralized communication, and version control to streamline teamwork.

- **Visual Brainstorming:** Early brainstorming sessions with writers and designers allow content and visuals to work in harmony, reinforcing the proposal's narrative and creating a cohesive message.

Common Barriers to Collaboration

1. Competing Priorities for Technical Staff

SMEs often juggle tight project deadlines, making it difficult to focus on proposals. The solution? Secure verbal commitments early and enlist leadership support to stress the importance of their input to the firm's success.

2. Misunderstood Roles

When teams assume proposal managers should handle everything, including technical content, the result is frustration and incomplete proposals. Use the kick-off meeting to clearly define roles and responsibilities so everyone understands their contributions.

3. Tight Deadlines

Compressed timelines can tempt teams to skip important steps, affecting proposal quality. Even under pressure, focus on essential processes like kick-off meetings, formal reviews, compliance checks, and daily updates to maintain quality and alignment.

Steps to Strengthen Collaboration

- **Build Trust and Rapport:** Relationships matter. Understand the work styles and personalities of your team, especially SMEs. Whether it's grabbing coffee or having informal check-ins, trust creates the foundation for effective collaboration.

- **Prepare Thoughtfully:** Research project details, past proposals, and SME backgrounds to ask meaningful questions. Providing clear agendas and expectations ahead of interviews ensures productive discussions and shows respect for their time.

- **Involve Leadership:** Executives play a critical role in driving accountability and emphasizing the importance of collaboration. Leadership involvement sends a clear message that every team member's input matters.

- **Streamline Communication:** Avoid overwhelming the team with unnecessary details. Instead, use concise daily updates or quick team check-ins to inform everyone without wasting time.

- **Incorporate Designers Early:** Engaging graphic designers from the outset makes sure visuals align with the content and narrative rather than becoming last-minute additions.

Why Collaboration Matters

Collaboration is not just a "nice to have" in proposal development; it's the backbone of success. Proposals created in isolation lack the depth, accuracy, and cohesion needed to win. Focusing on teamwork lets proposal teams leverage diverse skills, enhance quality, and improve win rates.

The bottom line? Proposals created through strong collaboration don't just look better; they perform better. When everyone—from SMEs to designers—contributes from the start, proposals become comprehensive and compelling and a powerful representation of the team's shared commitment to success.

Key Takeaways

- **Engage SMEs Early:** Their insights provide the technical depth and credibility your proposals need to stand out.

- **Hold Daily Check-Ins:** Quick, focused meetings ensure alignment, address roadblocks, and keep the team accountable.

- **Leverage Collaborative Tools:** Real-time platforms streamline editing, communication, and version control for seamless teamwork.

- **Align Visuals and Content:** Early involvement of graphic designers makes sure visuals amplify your win themes and simplify complex ideas.

- **Build Trust and Rapport:** Strong relationships foster open communication, improve collaboration, and lead to stronger proposals.

Chapter 9

Metrics of Impact

Defining Success in Proposals

It's tempting to define success only by whether you win the project. But here's the thing—winning is only one piece of the puzzle. True success goes beyond the outcome and includes the entire process that gets you there. Think of it like preparing a gourmet meal: the finished dish is important, sure, but the techniques, teamwork, and joy along the way make it a memorable experience.

So, what makes a proposal successful? It's not just about the final result. It's about team collaboration, enjoying the process, reducing stress on submission day, and ensuring thorough reviews. If your team works seamlessly together and feels accomplished by the end, you've achieved something remarkable. Like a well-rehearsed dance routine, a coordinated team delivers far better results than individuals working in isolation.

To measure success, we need to examine several key metrics: Outcome Metrics, Process Metrics, and Efficiency Metrics. Each plays a role in redefining what success looks like in proposal development.

The Building Blocks of Success

1. Outcome Metrics

Let's start with the obvious: did you win? Your win/loss record is a foundational metric for any proposal team. But success doesn't end there. Gathering client feedback through formal debriefs or informal discussions provides invaluable insights. What resonated with evaluators? What didn't? Think of this as the constructive critique after a presentation—it's how you refine and elevate your approach for future opportunities.

2. Process Metrics

Process metrics dive deeper into how your team collaborates and engages throughout the proposal lifecycle. Were your SMEs and reviewers contributing? Did the team meet deadlines without unnecessary chaos? A smooth, well-orchestrated process is often a strong predictor of success.

Stress management during submission is a critical indicator. Was submission day calm and organized, or was it a frantic scramble to meet the deadline? A stress-free submission day is a victory in itself. Planning and preparation upfront can dramatically reduce last-minute emergencies, creating a better experience for everyone involved.

The review phase is another pivotal area. Tracking the number and types of comments during reviews reveals the team's effectiveness. Fewer comments in later stages typically indicate higher quality and alignment early on. This progressive refinement ensures that your final product is polished and impactful.

3. Efficiency Metrics

Efficiency metrics focus on the resources and effort invested in a proposal. Tracking the hours spent on tasks—like writing, editing, layout, graphics, and production—offers valuable insights into how resources are allocated. Think of it like managing a household budget: knowing where your time and energy go helps you make smarter choices for the future.

Resource utilization is just as important. Were team members overworked? Did roles align with individual strengths? Finding the balance between challenging team members and overwhelming them is key. Efficient resource use produces better proposals and boosts team morale and retention.

Practical Steps for Measuring and Improving Success

Throughout the proposal lifecycle, there are critical points where you can assess success:

- **Kick-off Meeting:** Was the strategy clearly communicated? Did everyone understand their roles and responsibilities?
- **Content Development:** How efficiently were drafts completed? Were deadlines consistently met?
- **Submission:** Was submission day calm and stress-free? Did the team have ample time for quality checks?

By answering these questions, you can pinpoint strengths and weaknesses in your process. Each insight is an opportunity to improve.

Leveraging Data for Long-Term Success

Historical data is one of your greatest tools. Tracking metrics like labor hours, review cycles, and team engagement lets you refine your approach for future projects. For example, athletes review game footage to improve their performance, and proposal teams can learn from past efforts to continuously improve their game.

The Human Factor: Morale and Retention

Metrics are invaluable, but don't forget the human side of success. Team morale is a powerful indicator of long-term effectiveness. High stress and poor communication create disengaged teams. On the flip side, a team that feels valued and connected produces better results and enjoys the process along the way. Focus on collaboration, foster trust, and celebrate big and small wins to create a positive and productive work environment.

Rethinking What Success Looks Like

Success in proposal development isn't just about the win. It's about building a process that fosters collaboration, reduces stress, and makes the journey as rewarding as the destination. By focusing on metrics like hours spent, review quality, and team engagement, you can create a framework that supports consistent, high-quality proposals.

Remember, the journey matters just as much as the outcome. By redefining success to include the process and the people behind it, you'll build stronger teams, deliver better proposals, and set your firm up for long-term success.

Key Takeaways

- **Redefine Success:** Look beyond the final win to value the entire proposal process.

- **Foster Collaboration:** A well-aligned team with clear communication leads to better results.

- **Measure Effectively:** Track metrics like labor hours, review quality, and team engagement.

- **Focus on Team Morale:** A happy, engaged team produces higher-quality work and enjoys the process.

- **Learn and Adapt:** Use historical data and client feedback to continuously improve your proposals.

NOTES

Chapter 10

Step-by-Step to Success

Crafting a Compelling Proposal

A compelling proposal can feel like a monumental task, especially if you're new to the process. But think of it like constructing a house—you wouldn't lay the first brick without a solid foundation and a clear plan. Similarly, a winning proposal requires a structured approach that focuses on strategy, careful planning, and flawless execution. In this chapter, we'll walk through the essential steps to creating winning proposals, equipping you with the tools to succeed in this critical business activity.

Step 1: Strategy and Pre-Work

Before putting pen to paper, it's essential to define your objectives. Start by immersing yourself in the client's needs. This means analyzing the RFx, which is the blueprint of what the client expects. Look for details on their priorities, challenges, and evaluation criteria. To deepen your understanding, leverage tools like AI platforms to augment your research and explore the client's industry and past projects.

Once you've got a clear picture of the client's expectations, it's time to develop win themes—the key messages that spotlight your team's unique strengths. These themes should directly address the client's goals and challenges. Make sure every team member understands these themes and weaves them throughout their contributions to ensure a unified narrative. Think of win themes as the golden thread tying together all the elements of your proposal.

Next, create a framework to guide the entire proposal process. The compliance/responsibility matrix is an indispensable tool here. It maps out the RFx requirements, assigns ownership of each section, and outlines key elements like page limits, lead writers, and supporting team members. This matrix will act as your roadmap, making sure every requirement is addressed and nothing falls through the cracks.

An annotated outline is another must-have before you start writing. This detailed outline serves as the blueprint for your proposal, pinpointing where win themes, visuals, and compliance elements will be incorporated. This guide ensures your proposal remains strategic, persuasive, and client-focused from start to finish.

Step 2: Kick-Off Meeting

With your strategy defined and framework in place, the next step is the kick-off meeting. This is the moment to align your team and set the tone for collaboration. Share your win themes, compliance matrix, schedule, and annotated outline, making sure everyone understands their roles and deadlines.

Equip your team with the right tools. Collaborative platforms like Microsoft Teams or Google Workspace provide shared spaces for communication and document management, streamlining the development process.

Encourage open dialogue during the meeting. Create an environment where team members feel comfortable voicing concerns and sharing ideas. Sometimes, the best solutions come from unexpected places. If you anticipate challenges—like limited availability from SMEs—proactively plan contingencies to avoid delays.

Step 3: Management and Communication

Once the proposal is underway, maintaining clear and frequent communication is critical. Implement daily check-ins, often referred to as "play-of-the-day" meetings. These brief, focused sessions are perfect for tracking progress, identifying bottlenecks, and assigning next steps.

Keep detailed records of these meetings to ensure accountability and track progress against your compliance matrix. Proactive communication about schedule changes or shifts in client priorities will help keep everyone aligned and engaged.

Step 4: Content Development

This step is where most of the heavy lifting happens. Strong outlines are your best friend here. They provide writers with clear section objectives, win themes, and guidance on visuals, keeping them focused and aligned with the overall strategy.

While boilerplate content can save time, it must be tailored to the client's needs and preferences. Generic, cookie-cutter responses won't make an impression. Personalization is key to creating proposals that resonate.

Engage SMEs early and thoroughly. Schedule interviews armed with strategic questions to extract the technical insights you need. Your job is translating their expertise into client-centered narratives that speak to the client's challenges and goals.

Strive for an initial draft that's about 80% complete. This provides a solid foundation for revisions, leaving ample time to refine and polish the final submission. Address gaps or inconsistencies within the team before moving to the review phase to reduce rework.

Step 5: Reviews

A robust review process is a game changer for proposal quality. Implement distinct review cycles—pink team for content development, red team for strategy alignment, and gold team for final polish. Involving reviewers who weren't part of the initial writing process offers fresh perspectives and helps catch errors or inconsistencies that others might miss.

Centralize feedback using tools like Adobe Share to ensure clarity and transparency. Collecting all comments in one document makes tracking revisions and implementing changes easier.

Step 6: Submission, Close-Out, and Debrief

As submission day approaches, perform rigorous quality checks to confirm compliance with RFP requirements. If time or resources are tight, consider using AI tools to streamline compliance reviews.

Test the submission platform in advance to avoid technical issues that could derail your hard work. Double-check every detail to ensure your proposal is submitted flawlessly.

After submission, conduct a thorough debrief with your team. Analyze what went well, what could have been improved, and any lessons learned. These insights are invaluable for refining your process and improving future proposals.

Don't forget to celebrate your team's efforts—recognizing contributions boosts morale and keeps your team motivated for the next challenge.

The Bigger Picture

A compelling proposal is a nuanced process that requires thoughtful strategy, careful planning, and seamless execution at every stage. While all steps are important, the content development phase often has the most significant impact on the proposal's success. Investing time and effort here will pay off in proposals that meet client expectations and stand out in a competitive market.

A great proposal is built on a strong process. Each stage contributes to the quality and impact of the final submission. By following these structured steps, you'll create proposals that shine and set your team apart.

Key Takeaways

- **Structured Processes Win:** Following clear, repeatable steps ensures alignment, quality, and efficiency.

- **Content Development is Key:** Focus your efforts here to craft proposals that are impactful and client-centered.

- **Early Engagement Matters:** Involve SMEs, designers, and reviewers early and often to create cohesive, compelling proposals.

- **Learn and Evolve:** Use debriefs and lessons learned to continuously refine your process and improve future outcomes.

NOTES

Chapter 11

Strategies for Success

Boosting Win Rates and Reducing Stress

Proposal development often feels like climbing a mountain. Tight deadlines, complex requirements, and the weight of expectations can overwhelm even experienced professionals. But it doesn't have to be this way. In this chapter, we'll explore actionable strategies to boost your win rates while helping you breathe easier during proposal season. With the right tools, training, and planning, you can create a streamlined, repeatable process that delivers consistent results without the stress.

Standardized Training: Building a Unified Team

One of the best ways to reduce stress during proposal development is to ensure that everyone on your team—coordinators, writers, designers, SMEs, and reviewers—is aligned and understands the process. Training is like establishing a shared language for your team. When everyone knows what to expect, chaos transforms into collaboration.

Start by hosting regular training sessions that walk team members through your proposal process, breaking it down into clear stages and best practices. Equip them with easy-to-use templates, checklists, and guides. As athletes practice before a big game, a well-trained proposal team performs better when they understand their roles and expectations.

During kick-off meetings, reinforce the importance of these processes to ensure everyone is on the same page. Highlight how following these steps helps the entire team, streamlining the process and setting the foundation for success.

Leveraging Technology for Efficiency

Today, technology can be a game changer for enhancing the quality of your proposals and the efficiency of the process. Tools like Grammarly and AI-driven content generators can save valuable time and reduce stress. Imagine tackling the daunting task of drafting a proposal from scratch. Now, picture a tool that delivers an initial draft that's already 80% complete. That's the magic of technology in action.

Grammarly helps ensure your writing is polished, professional, and free of errors. AI content generators can produce initial drafts for project descriptions or technical sections, giving you a head start and allowing more time for customization. Graphic design software, meanwhile, brings your proposals to life with visuals that make key messages pop and improve overall readability.

By incorporating these tools into your workflow, you can shift your focus to refining strategy and creating tailored content, leaving the tedious groundwork to technology.

Verifying Compliance at Every Stage

Non-compliance with RFx requirements is one of the most common and costly mistakes in proposal development. It can derail your efforts before your proposal even gets reviewed. That's why a compliance matrix is an essential tool—it serves as your guide to ensure every requirement is met.

Incorporate compliance checks into every stage of your process, from initial outline creation to the final review. Reference your compliance matrix during pink, red, and gold team reviews to confirm that all criteria are addressed. Think of it as a checklist that keeps your proposal on track. Conducting a final compliance check before submission ensures that no details are missed, giving you confidence that your proposal meets all the requirements.

Effective Planning: The Antidote to Stress

Stress often arises when teams feel unprepared or rushed to meet deadlines. *The solution?* **Effective planning.** A comprehensive plan, like a responsibility matrix, completed for the kick-off meeting outlines deadlines, specific tasks, and individual responsibilities and is the roadmap for your team. Everyone knows what they should do and when.

For example, during the pink team draft phase, aim to produce content that is close to the quality you expect for the red team review. Use past proposals as go-bys and integrate AI tools to tailor your content to the specific opportunity. This reduces the amount of rework required later and lets reviewers focus on strategy rather than correcting basic issues.

Time Management: Staying on Track

Time is one of your most valuable resources during proposal development and managing it well can mean the difference between a seamless process and a chaotic scramble. Start by tracking how much time your team spends on writing, editing, and graphics. Tools like Clockify can provide insights into where time is being spent and find ways to improve.

Create protected time blocks in your calendar dedicated to high-priority tasks, and treat them as if they were essential meetings. These focused sessions reduce distractions and keep you on track. Focus on tasks with the greatest impact on the proposal's success, such as crafting compelling win themes or perfecting the section worth the most points.

A Day in a Stress-Free Proposal Process

Imagine this: Your team begins a new proposal fully prepared, thanks to regular training sessions that have established a standardized process. AI tools have generated an 80% complete first draft, aligned with your win themes and client goals. Daily check-ins keep the team in sync, while compliance checks ensure every detail is addressed. By submission day, the proposal is polished, aligned, and ready to go—leaving everyone calm, confident, and ready for the next opportunity.

This isn't just a dream. It's the reality you can achieve by applying the strategies outlined in this chapter. Standardized training, cutting-edge tools, and careful planning are your keys to reducing stress and consistently delivering high-quality proposals.

Key Takeaways

- **Train Your Team on a Proven Process:** Consistency and shared understanding improve collaboration and reduce stress.

- **Leverage Technology:** Tools like Grammarly and AI content generators streamline drafts, leaving more time for strategic refinement.

- **Verify Compliance at Every Step:** A compliance matrix ensures all requirements are met, avoiding costly oversights.

- **Plan Effectively:** Strong planning minimizes rework, saves time, and keeps the team focused on priorities.

- **Use Time Wisely:** Protect your schedule with focused time blocks and focus on high-impact tasks for maximum efficiency.

NOTES

Chapter 12

Client-Centric Proposals

Understanding Needs for Better Outcomes

When developing a proposal, it's important to see it as more than just a document. A proposal is a conversation—a bridge connecting your team to the client's aspirations, challenges, and goals. The success of your proposal lies in how well you understand these factors and translate them into a tailored, compelling response. This chapter explores how to transform your proposals from static responses into dynamic, client-focused narratives that make an impact.

Understanding Client Needs: The Cornerstone of Success

Understanding your client's needs is the foundation of effective proposal writing. A winning proposal doesn't just check the boxes of the RFx—it resonates with the client, addressing their specific goals and pain points. It positions your team as more than a vendor; you become a trusted partner who deeply understands their unique challenges. This level of alignment sets you apart and pushes your team to the forefront of the selection process.

A generic, cookie-cutter approach won't do. Tailored solutions make your proposal stand out, showing the client that you've taken the time to understand their priorities and deliver strategies that work specifically for them.

Gathering Client Insights

Engage Your Subject Matter Experts

SMEs are often your closest connection to the client's world. Their insights are invaluable for understanding the client's needs, concerns, and objectives. By asking targeted questions during your SME interviews, you can uncover key details that shape your proposal strategy. For instance, past interactions with the client might reveal preferences, expectations, or even areas where previous companies fell short—giving your proposal a strategic edge.

Dive Into Client Research

SME input is important, but it's only part of the puzzle. Complement this with in-depth client research. Explore their website, annual reports, press releases, and social media channels to get a well-rounded view of their mission, values, and priorities. Whenever possible, participate in pre-proposal engagements, such as client meetings or site visits. These opportunities provide firsthand insights into their decision-making processes and the outcomes they value most.

Tailoring Your Proposal

A Strong First Impression: Customizing the Cover Letter

The cover letter is the handshake of your proposal—it sets the tone and makes your first impression. Use it to immediately convey your understanding of the client's goals and challenges. Highlight how your team's unique approach addresses these needs and why you're the right choice for the project. End with a confident call to action, reinforcing your commitment to providing value and becoming their partner in success.

Personalizing Key Sections

Customization doesn't stop with the cover letter. Every section of your proposal should reflect the client's priorities and preferences.

- **Executive Summary:** Use this section to clearly articulate how your solution solves the client's most pressing challenges. Speak their language and emphasize the unique benefits your team offers.

- **Resumes and Team Bios:** Highlight relevant experience that aligns directly with the client's industry or project. Showcase your team's expertise in a way that builds confidence in their ability to deliver.

By aligning every element of the proposal to the client's needs, you create a submission that feels personal and tailored—not just another generic response.

Building Relationships for Stronger Proposals

Trust as the Foundation

Proposals don't exist in a vacuum—they're part of a broader relationship-building effort. Trust is critical to this process. Show genuine interest in the client's long-term success, not just the immediate project. Proactive communication and a clear understanding of their objectives will show your dedication to their needs.

Personalized Proposals

Reference specific conversations, insights, or details from earlier engagements in your proposal. This level of personalization reassures clients that you've been listening and that your team truly cares. It's these touches that turn a good proposal into a great one.

Ongoing Engagement

Even after the RFx is released, stay engaged with the client. Ask clarifying questions, seek feedback, and remain adaptable. Be sure to follow to rules of engagement identified in your RFx. You don't want to get thrown out before you submit. This continuous dialogue ensures your proposal evolves alongside the client's needs and reinforces your commitment to their success.

Applying Client Insights Effectively

Develop Customized Content

When your insights are applied effectively, your proposal becomes a compelling narrative that speaks directly to the client's priorities. For example, if innovation or sustainability are critical to them, ensure these themes are front and center in your technical approach. Use specific examples and practices to show your expertise in these areas.

Include What Matters

Clarity is key—focus on what's most relevant to the client. Avoid overwhelming evaluators with unnecessary details. Instead, present the information that aligns with their expectations and objectives, making your proposal easier to evaluate and more impactful.

A Client-Centered Approach Wins Proposals

Understanding your client isn't just an initial step—it's a mindset that drives the entire proposal process. This deep understanding lets you craft submissions that resonate, showing your expertise and alignment with their goals. By leveraging client insights and building trust, your proposals go beyond generic responses—they become persuasive conversations that position your team as the ideal partner.

Winning proposals aren't about filling out templates; they're about creating something meaningful and relevant to the client. When your submissions reflect a genuine understanding of their needs, they stand out and build the foundation for successful partnerships.

Key Takeaways

- **Understanding the Client is Essential:** Deeply knowing your client's goals and challenges ensures your proposal is relevant and compelling.

- **Gather Insights from Multiple Sources:** Leverage SMEs, conduct thorough client research, and participate in pre-proposal engagements.

- **Tailor Every Section:** Customize the cover letter, executive summary, technical approach, resumes, etc., to reflect client priorities.

- **Relationships Matter:** Strong relationships and trust-building efforts positively influence proposal outcomes.

NOTES

Chapter 13

The Art of Persuasion

Storytelling in Proposals

Proposals play a vital role in communication. They provide an opportunity to highlight your company's unique strengths and offerings. Unfortunately, many professionals view proposals as mere formalities filled with technical jargon and lengthy compliance checklists. But what if your proposal could be more than just another document? What if it could tell a compelling story that resonates deeply with your client? This is where the art of storytelling comes into play.

What Does Storytelling in Proposals Mean?

When you think of storytelling, images of grand adventures or emotional tales might come to mind. While proposals don't require the drama of a novel, they benefit from the core principles of storytelling. In a proposal, storytelling is about weaving a narrative that reflects your client's goals, challenges, and vision for success. It's not about inventing a fictional tale; it's about customizing your message to feel relevant, personal, and uniquely crafted for the client.

At its heart, storytelling in proposals centers on creating a connection—showing your clients that you not only understand their needs but that your team is the perfect partner to help them meet their goals.

Why Storytelling Matters in Decision-Making

Storytelling has a unique power: it engages both the logical and emotional sides of decision-making. While logical elements—like technical knowledge and compliance—show your ability to meet the RFx's requirements, the emotional side builds trust and credibility. It's the emotional connection that leaves evaluators with a lasting impression and sets your proposal apart from the competition.

The Building Blocks of a Great Proposal Story

A Clear Vision

Every great story begins with a clear vision. In proposals, this means aligning your content with the client's goals. If sustainability is a key priority, for example, your narrative should highlight innovative solutions that reduce environmental impact while meeting technical and financial goals. Painting a vivid picture of success—one that matches your client's aspirations—lays the foundation for a winning proposal.

Tailored Solutions

No two clients are the same, and your proposals shouldn't be either. Tailor your solutions to address the client's specific challenges and priorities. This customized approach shows you've done your homework and understand what matters most to them. A tailored narrative showcases your knowledge and builds confidence that your team is uniquely equipped to meet their needs.

Compelling Proof Points

The best stories are backed by evidence. Use compelling proof points—like case studies, past project successes, client quotes, and measurable results—to confirm your claims. These examples give evaluators concrete reassurance that your team has the skills and experience to deliver. Proof points aren't just about bragging rights; they're about building trust.

The Client as the Hero

In every great story, the hero takes center stage. In proposals, the hero is your client. Your narrative should focus on how your team supports the client in achieving their vision. Use language that centers their goals and frames your team as the reliable, skilled partner helping them succeed. This approach shifts the focus from what you offer to **what the client gains**—*a critical distinction in making your proposal stand out.*

Storytelling in Action: A Case Study

Let's bring this idea to life with an example. Imagine a firm responding to an RFP for a public transportation infrastructure project. Instead of delivering a dry, technical proposal focused only on specifications, the firm chose to frame its narrative around the community impact of the project.

Their proposal described how their work would enhance safety, reduce traffic congestion, and improve the quality of life for residents. They backed this narrative with photos of community engagement efforts, testimonials from past clients, and measurable outcomes from similar projects.

This approach didn't just highlight the firm's technical skills; it created a story of transformation. By focusing on the broader impact of their work, they connected with the client's values and priorities, ultimately securing the winning bid.

Techniques for Integrating Storytelling into Proposals

Start with the Client's Vision

Begin by identifying what success looks like for the client. Use their own language—straight from the RFx or previous conversations—to show alignment and understanding. Let their vision guide the structure and tone of your proposal.

Include Relevant Examples

Strengthen your narrative with real-world examples. Use case studies, testimonials, and metrics to illustrate your knowledge and show that you understand the client's challenges. These examples should reinforce your message and make it relatable.

Enhance with Visuals

Visuals are a powerful tool for storytelling. Use charts, infographics, and photographs to bring your narrative to life. Make sure every visual supports your story and aligns with the client's goals, adding clarity and impact to your proposal.

Maintain a Consistent Voice

Your proposal should speak with one voice—a voice that is clear, empathetic, and aligned with the client's priorities. Avoid jargon that might confuse or alienate your audience. Instead, focus on concise, compelling language that builds connection and trust.

Why Storytelling Wins Proposals

The answer is simple: storytelling makes your proposal memorable. In a competitive landscape, where evaluators sift through countless submissions, a well-told story stands out. It engages decision-makers on both a logical and emotional level, creating a proposal that resonates and inspires action.

The Value of Storytelling

The power of storytelling in proposals lies in its ability to customize your message and connect with your client. A great proposal goes beyond meeting RFx requirements; it reflects the client's story and positions your team as the partner who can help bring it to life. By incorporating storytelling into your proposals, you're not just improving your chances of winning—you're building the foundation for meaningful, long-term client relationships.

Key Takeaways

- **Make the Client the Hero:** Focus your narrative on the client's goals, framing your role as a trusted partner.

- **Customize Every Proposal:** Tailor your content and solutions to align with the client's unique challenges and priorities.

- **Use Proof Points Effectively:** Strengthen your story with case studies, testimonials, and measurable results that confirm your claims.

- **Enhance with Visuals:** Incorporate impactful visuals that reinforce your narrative and highlight key benefits.

- **Maintain a Clear, Consistent Voice:** Avoid jargon and focus on empathetic, client-centered communication.

NOTES

Chapter 14

Resource Mastery

Managing Time and Team During Proposals

In proposal development, how you manage your resources can make or break your project. Time and team members are your most valuable assets; using them effectively can mean the difference between success and failure.

Proposal development is as much an art as it is a science. For those stepping into management roles or tackling proposals without formal training, the intricacies of resource management might feel overwhelming. However, mastering this skill leads to improved collaboration, reduced stress, and ultimately, the timely delivery of high-quality proposals that win work.

Understanding the Time Commitment

The first step in resource management is understanding the time commitment each proposal requires. Proposals vary widely—from straightforward qualifications to intricate technical submissions. Tracking the time spent on tasks like writing, editing, designing, and reviewing will help you build a database of benchmarks.

Over time, this data becomes a powerful tool for estimating future projects and planning effectively. It will also help you identify where your team's efforts yield the most value. For example, writing and editing are typically high-impact activities that can elevate the overall quality of the proposal, but obsessing over minor details often adds little value.

Recognizing your team's "point of no return"—the moment when more effort no longer improves the final product—lets you allocate resources where they matter most and keeps projects on track.

Starting Strong: The Kick-Off Meeting

Think of the kick-off meeting as the foundation for your proposal. Without a solid start, the rest of the process risks instability. This meeting is your opportunity to align the team, establish expectations, and build a sense of shared purpose.

During the kick-off meeting:

- Define roles and responsibilities for SMEs, writers, editors, designers, and reviewers.
- Decide the key milestones, including deadlines for drafts, reviews, and final submissions.
- Emphasize the importance of meeting deadlines and sticking to the process.

A strong kick-off ensures clarity, reduces confusion, and fosters collaboration. When team members feel included and understand their roles, they are more likely to commit to the proposal's success.

Prioritizing Tasks Across Multiple Proposals

Managing multiple proposals with overlapping deadlines requires a structured approach. Prioritization is key:

- Focus on proposals with the closest deadlines.

- Assess the progress of each proposal to identify which ones need more resources.

- Account for complexity; more intricate proposals often require earlier attention, even if their deadlines are further away.

This approach ensures that no proposal is neglected and that all submissions maintain a high standard of quality.

Communicating Realistic Expectations

Communication is the cornerstone of resource management. Establish realistic timelines for each stage of the proposal process, from first drafts to review cycles like pink, red, and gold team reviews.

Regular check-ins with your team maintain accountability and provide opportunities to address challenges before they escalate. Setting achievable deadlines fosters a cooperative environment and reduces stress, letting team members focus on producing their best work.

Using Tools for Resource Allocation

Technology can streamline resource management and improve efficiency. Tools like Clockify or other time-tracking software let you monitor how time is allocated across various tasks, helping you identify inefficiencies.

Project management platforms like Microsoft Teams, Trello, Asana, or Monday.com keep your workflow organized and make sure everyone knows what needs to be done and when. These tools improve communication, reduce the risk of missed deadlines, and help allocate resources where they're needed most.

Leveraging Play-of-the-Day Meetings

Daily play-of-the-day meetings are an excellent way to stay aligned. These brief check-ins focus on the following:

- Status updates for key tasks.

- Addressing roadblocks in real time.

- Realigning priorities based on progress and deadlines.

Play-of-the-day meetings foster a culture of responsiveness and adaptability, keeping the team connected and the project on track.

Practical Tips for Resource Management

Here are some tips to enhance resource management in your proposal process:

- **Understand Your Hours:** Track time spent on different types of proposals to develop accurate benchmarks for future planning.

- **Focus on High-Impact Tasks:** Direct resources toward writing and editing, where they make the biggest difference. Avoid spending excessive time on tasks with diminishing returns, like making the design or layout perfect.

- **Enforce Accountability:** Use tools and regular check-ins to ensure team members meet their responsibilities.

- **Plan Ahead:** Prioritize based on deadlines and complexity and establish clear milestones to keep all proposals on track.

The Keys to Successful Resource Management

Effective resource management is both an art and a science. By understanding the time requirements of proposals, focusing on high-value activities, and fostering clear communication, you create an environment that promotes productivity and reduces stress.

Whether you're handling one proposal or juggling several, the strategies outlined here will help you manage resources effectively, empower your team, and deliver exceptional results.

The bottom line?

Resource management isn't just a skill; it's the foundation of an efficient and successful proposal process.

Key Takeaways

- **Track Time for Accuracy:** Record how long each step of the proposal process takes, from writing to reviews, to improve future planning.

- **Focus on Value-Added Activities:** Prioritize high-impact tasks like crafting compelling narratives and meeting compliance requirements.

- **Focus on and Plan:** Tackle proposals based on deadlines and complexity, allocating resources to avoid last-minute scrambles.

- **Leverage Technology:** Use time-tracking tools like Clockify and project management platforms like Microsoft Teams to improve efficiency and accountability.

- **Communicate Clearly:** Begin with a strong kick-off meeting, maintain daily check-ins, and set realistic expectations to keep the team aligned and productive.

NOTES

Chapter 15

Strategic Alignment

Enhancing Proposal Quality and Relevance

Proposals are more than just a response to contract requirements—they're a critical opportunity to showcase your company's vision, knowledge, and values. Aligning proposals with your firm's strategic goals can elevate their quality and set you apart from competitors. But how do you ensure your proposals reflect both the client's needs and your company's larger ambitions? Let's break it down.

Proposals as Strategic Tools

Proposals aren't just technical documents—they're strategic storytelling tools. When aligned with your company's goals, they do more than meet the client's needs; they communicate how your firm's priorities complement the client's objectives. For example, if your company focuses on sustainability, your proposals should highlight environmentally friendly practices and showcase relevant successes. Instead of listing your services, *show how your commitment to sustainability adds value to the client's project*. By aligning your proposals this way, you elevate their quality and establish your firm as a trusted partner.

Why Alignment Matters

Every company has strategic goals, whether it's expanding into new markets, focusing on certain project types, or reinforcing a mission. Proposals aligned with these goals help win projects and strengthen your firm's identity. Take a company aiming to grow in sustainable design, for example. If you're pursuing a project with similar objectives, your proposal should consistently showcase your expertise in this area. Include examples like case studies of past energy-efficient designs or innovative green solutions. By doing so, you show your alignment with the client's priorities and underscore your firm's mission.

Steps to Ensure Alignment

1. Hold a Kick-Off Meeting

Before writing, gather your team for a kick-off meeting to set the tone. Use this session to answer critical questions:

- How does this opportunity align with our strategic goals?
- What key messages should this proposal convey?
- What makes us uniquely suited for this client and project?

This meeting ensures everyone is aligned from the start, giving the proposal a clear intent and purpose.

2. Use a Strategic Alignment Matrix

A Strategic Alignment Matrix is a practical tool to connect client priorities with your firm's goals. Create a table with *client needs in one column* and *your company's strengths in another*. For each priority, identify examples that show your ability to meet the client's needs while advancing your strategic objectives. This approach keeps your proposal focused and ensures your responses are both relevant and impactful.

3. Learn from Feedback

After submitting a proposal, take time to reflect. Hold a debrief meeting and ask:

- Did our proposal align with our company's goals?
- Were there opportunities to better emphasize our strategic message?
- What feedback did we receive about how well we aligned with the client's priorities?

This process isn't just about looking back—it's about learning and improving for the future.

4. Build a Knowledge Repository

Create a knowledge repository to store insights from past proposals, successful case studies, and lessons learned. This organized library becomes a go-to resource for aligning content with your strategic objectives, making future proposals faster to develop and more consistent in messaging.

Embedding Alignment Throughout the Proposal

Once you've set the foundation for alignment, weave your strategy into every section of the proposal:

- **Cover Letter/Executive Summary:** This is your first opportunity to connect your mission with the client's needs. Highlight how your firm's values and knowledge make you the ideal partner.

- **Technical Sections:** Go beyond listing methods. Explain how your approach reflects your strategic focus, whether it's sustainability, innovation, or another core goal.

- **Team Bios:** Showcase team members' experience that aligns with the client's concerns, emphasizing knowledge that supports both project requirements and your firm's mission.

Embedding alignment consistently throughout the proposal strengthens your message and reinforces your value to the client.

Balancing Strategic Goals with Client Needs

While aligning proposals with your strategic goals is essential, it's equally important to address the client's immediate requirements. Focus on opportunities that align with your long-term goals but tailor your content to meet the client's specific needs. Striking this balance ensures that your proposal is both relevant and forward-thinking.

Final Thoughts

When proposals align with your company's strategic goals, they shift from routine submissions into powerful business tools. You meet the RFx requirements and emphasize your firm's broader vision and values. Aligned proposals don't just secure projects—they tell a bigger story about who you are and what your firm stands for. This approach helps your proposals stand out in a competitive market, building relationships and creating opportunities for growth. Remember, a well-aligned proposal is more than a document; it's a chance to showcase your identity, values, and ambitions in a way that resonates with clients.

Key Takeaways

- **Understand Your Goals:** Ensure the proposal team is aware of your company's strategic priorities to create more impactful submissions.

- **Use Alignment Tools:** Hold strategic discussions and use tools like alignment matrixes to connect client needs with company goals.

- **Learn from Past Submissions:** Regularly review proposals and client feedback to identify gaps and opportunities for stronger alignment.

- **Embed Strategy Throughout:** Integrate your strategic messages across all proposal sections, from the cover letter to resumes.

- **Balance Long- and Short-Term Goals:** Address the client's immediate needs while aligning with your company's long-term goals for a comprehensive and compelling proposal.

Chapter 16

The Cost of Failure

Understanding Implications of Poor Proposal Development

Proposals are the gateway to lucrative projects and a chance to show your firm's value, vision, and expertise. In industries where decisions are made based on value rather than price alone, the quality of your proposal can determine success or failure. Yet too many professionals underestimate the stakes, resulting in poorly developed proposals that lead to missed opportunities and ripple effects far beyond lost revenue.

The Consequences of Rushing the Proposal Process

Picture this: your firm sets its sights on a $50 million federal infrastructure project. The team is enthusiastic, confident in its technical capabilities, and certain this is a perfect fit. But instead of dedicating the necessary time and resources to crafting a thoughtful, strategic proposal, the process is rushed. Steps like a go/no-go analysis are skipped, and the end result is a submission that fails to communicate your firm's unique value.

The outcome? *Wasted resources, a missed opportunity, and a hit to your reputation.* This cautionary tale underscores a hard truth: neglecting strategic proposal development isn't just a lost contract—this setback can affect future opportunities, relationships, and growth.

The Financial Implications of Poor Proposals

The financial fallout from a poorly crafted proposal can be staggering. Let's break it down. Your firm invests hundreds of hours and thousands of dollars into developing a submission, only for it to be disqualified due to compliance errors. The immediate loss of the contract stings, but the real damage runs deeper.

Disqualified proposals drain your resources, limiting your ability to invest in future opportunities. Worse, they can tarnish your reputation. If your firm develops a reputation as an unreliable or inconsistent partner, it becomes harder to secure future work—affecting your long-term revenue and ability to retain top talent. Poor proposal development doesn't just cost you a project; it weakens your standing in the market.

The Go/No-Go Decision: A Key Safeguard

So, how can you avoid these pitfalls? It starts with a thorough go/no-go analysis, a critical step that evaluates whether a proposal is worth pursuing. Ask yourself key questions:

- Is this project a strategic priority for our firm?
- Does it align with our knowledge and strengths?
- Do we have the resources to deliver a high-quality proposal and fulfill the project requirements?

By taking the time to assess these factors upfront, your firm can focus its energy on opportunities that are both winnable and aligned with your long-term goals.

Building a Proven Proposal Process

A structured, proven proposal process is your next line of defense against poor outcomes. Start with a clear strategy that aligns with client priorities and use well-defined steps to guide your team:

- **Kick-off Meetings:** Establish roles, responsibilities, and timelines to ensure everyone knows what's expected.

- **Pink, Red, and Gold Team Reviews:** Refine your messaging and verify compliance through iterative reviews.

- **Compliance Checks:** Before submission, ensure all RFP requirements are addressed to eliminate disqualification risks.

This systematic approach reduces errors, enhances quality, and ensures your proposals meet client expectations while reflecting your firm's strategic goals.

Learning from Past Submissions

Every proposal—win or lose—is a learning opportunity. After each submission, conduct a debrief to identify what worked, what didn't, and where you can improve:

- Were there compliance issues?

- Did the proposal effectively address the client's evaluation criteria?

- What feedback did the client provide about the submission?

By analyzing past performance and implementing feedback, you create a feedback loop that strengthens your proposal process. This continuous improvement builds confidence, consistency, and higher-quality submissions.

The Role of Collaboration and Communication

A successful proposal is always a team effort. Strong collaboration and communication are essential to ensuring all parts of the submission align with the client's needs and your firm's goals.

- Engage SMEs early to provide accurate, relevant content.

- Establish daily check-ins—like quick "Play-of-the-Day" meetings—to address roadblocks and maintain alignment.

- Foster a culture of accountability so every team member understands the importance of their contributions.

By keeping everyone on the same page, you reduce errors and maximize your team's efficiency.

The Importance of Strategic Focus

While the temptation to pursue every opportunity can be strong, casting too wide a net dilutes your resources and reduces your chances of success. Instead, maintain a strategic focus.

Concentrate on high-impact pursuits that align with your firm's strengths and priorities. By targeting fewer opportunities with greater precision, your firm can dedicate the time and energy required to produce compelling, high-quality proposals that stand out.

The Costs of Poor Proposal Development

The costs of poorly developed proposals go beyond a single missed project. Non-compliance, lack of strategic focus, or failure to articulate your firm's value can tarnish your reputation, erode client trust, and hinder growth. Proposals that don't meet the mark don't just cost you revenue—they threaten your firm's long-term position in the market.

Proactive Measures for Success

Here's the good news: by taking proactive measures, your firm can avoid these costly pitfalls. Conduct go/no-go analyses, invest in a structured proposal process, learn from past submissions, and focus on collaboration. These actions don't just prevent failure—they pave the way for greater success.

Quality Over Quantity

The takeaway is clear: in the world of proposals, quality always trumps quantity. Poor proposal development can cost millions in missed opportunities, but a thoughtful, structured approach can lead to consistent wins and stronger client relationships.

By dedicating the necessary time and resources, aligning your proposals with strategic goals, and fostering a culture of collaboration, your firm will navigate the competitive landscape with confidence. Invest in getting it right, and you'll see the rewards—not just in contracts won but in the lasting reputation of your firm as a reliable, value-driven partner.

Key Takeaways

- **Conduct Thorough Go/No-Go Analyses:** Evaluate opportunities to ensure alignment with your firm's strategic priorities, knowledge, and resources.

- **Establish a Proven Proposal Process:** Use structured steps like kick-off meetings, iterative reviews, and compliance checks to enhance quality and accuracy.

- **Learn from Past Submissions:** Debrief after each proposal to identify strengths, weaknesses, and opportunities for improvement.

- **Focus on Collaboration and Communication:** Engage SMEs early, hold regular check-ins, and foster accountability to align team efforts and avoid errors.

- **Focus on Strategic Opportunities:** Concentrate resources on high-impact pursuits to increase your chances of success and maximize value.

NOTES

Chapter 17

Tech-Savvy Proposals

The Role of Technology in Proposals

In proposal development, standing still isn't an option. With competition intensifying and deadlines getting tighter, proposal professionals are turning to technology to streamline their workflows and gain a competitive edge. Technology has become a transformative force, redefining how proposals are created, reviewed, and submitted. In this chapter, we'll dive into how technology enhances efficiency, elevates quality, and enables unparalleled customization—turning proposals into powerful tools that win work.

Technology: Your Partner in the Process

Think of technology as the sous chef in your proposal kitchen. Just as a chef relies on state-of-the-art gadgets to create a standout dish, proposal professionals must leverage modern tools to craft submissions that captivate clients. Technology doesn't replace expertise; it complements it, enabling you to deliver polished, compelling proposals that rise above the competition.

The Core Functions of Technology in Proposals

At its heart, technology enhances three key areas in proposal development: efficiency, quality, and customization.

1. Enhancing Efficiency

Technology speeds up the proposal process by centralizing information and streamlining workflows. Tools like project management software and Customer Relationship Management (CRM) systems let teams quickly access important data, such as client preferences or past project details, cutting down on time spent searching for resources.

2. Ensuring Quality Control

Writing aids like Grammarly and PerfectIt make sure your proposals are error-free and polished. These tools act as a second set of eyes, catching mistakes that might slip through even the most careful reviews. By automating grammar and style checks, they free up time for teams to focus on refining strategy and messaging.

3. Enabling Customization

AI-powered tools take customization to the next level. These technologies can analyze historical data and client preferences to help teams draft tailored content that speaks directly to the client's needs. By delivering personalized, targeted responses, AI tools boost the impact of your proposals and increase your chances of winning.

Essential Tools for Proposal Development

Customer Relationship Management Systems

CRMs serve as your proposal command center. Platforms like Deltek, Salesforce, or HubSpot organize all client and project information in one place, making it easy to monitor opportunities, track past interactions, and find patterns in what resonates with clients. With these insights, teams can craft proposals that build on earlier successes and address client priorities with precision.

Content Databases

Imagine having a fully searchable library of past proposals, resumes, and project details at your fingertips. Content databases provide just that, saving teams time while ensuring consistency and brand alignment across submissions. These tools let you reuse proven language and templates, enhancing efficiency and quality.

Writing and Editing Tools

Tools like Grammarly and PerfectIt are essential for automating tedious editing tasks. They catch grammatical errors, ensure adherence to style guidelines, and polish the overall tone of your proposal. With less time spent on copyediting, teams can focus on the bigger picture—creating content that connects with clients.

AI-Powered Tools

AI tools, like ChatGPT and Perplexity, are the brainstorming partners of the future. These technologies can generate initial drafts, conduct research, and even suggest tailored content based on client needs. While AI is a valuable starting point, the human touch remains essential to refine these drafts into compelling, client-focused narratives.

The Future of Technology in Proposals

Evolving AI Capabilities

AI is evolving rapidly, opening new doors for proposal development. Imagine tools that provide real-time client insights or platforms that enable seamless collaboration with live editing suggestions. Staying informed and adaptable will be key to leveraging these advancements and maintaining a competitive edge.

Innovative tools like proposal automation platforms and visualization software are set to revolutionize workflows. Integrating CRMs, content databases, and writing tools into a single streamlined platform could dramatically enhance efficiency and consistency. Firms that adopt these technologies early will position themselves as industry leaders.

Best Practices for Leveraging Technology

- **Invest in the Right Tools:** Identify specific challenges within your proposal process and choose tools that address those needs directly.

- **Maintain Up-to-Date Databases:** Regularly refresh your content to ensure it reflects your firm's current capabilities and expertise.

- **Combine AI with Human Expertise:** Use AI for drafting and analysis, but rely on your team's insights and creativity to personalize and refine proposals.

- **Train Your Team:** Equip your team with the skills needed to maximize the potential of these tools through regular training and knowledge-sharing.

Embracing Technology for Proposal Excellence

Technology is no longer a helpful addition to the proposal process—it's an essential partner. From streamlining workflows to delivering client-focused content, the right tools can transform your approach to proposal development. By embracing technology, you're not just keeping pace with industry demands but setting yourself apart in a crowded, competitive market.

A Partner, Not a Replacement

Technology isn't here to replace creativity or technical expertise but to elevate them. The firms that embrace technological innovation can enhance efficiency, deliver higher-quality proposals, and differentiate themselves in a competitive landscape. By combining the power of technology with the unique insights of your team, you'll create proposals that resonate with clients and win work. So, embrace the tools and set the stage for proposal excellence.

Key Takeaways

- **Enhance Efficiency with Centralized Systems:** CRMs and content databases streamline workflows by organizing client information, project details, and past proposals in one accessible location.

- **Ensure Quality with Writing Aids:** Tools like Grammarly and PerfectIt automate grammar and style checks, letting teams focus on refining strategy and messaging.

- **Leverage AI for Customization:** AI-powered tools like ChatGPT and Perplexity enable faster drafting, tailored responses, and client-focused content creation to enhance proposal quality.

- **Adopt Emerging Technologies:** Stay ahead of the curve with advanced platforms like proposal automation tools and visualization software to improve collaboration and efficiency.

- **Combine Technology with Expertise:** Technology accelerates processes, but the creativity, technical insight, and strategic thinking of your team remain essential for crafting standout proposals.

NOTES

Chapter 18

Continuous Growth

Improving Proposal Skills Beyond Initial Development

As proposal professionals, it's easy to feel a sense of accomplishment after mastering the basics of the job. But here's the reality: in a fast-evolving field, standing still isn't an option. The business landscape is constantly shifting, and staying relevant requires continuous growth and skill improvement. So, how do you develop your proposal skills beyond the initial training? Let's explore strategies to ensure your learning journey remains impactful, dynamic, and even enjoyable.

Continuing the Proposal Journey: Building Skills Beyond the Basics

Mastering proposal development is not a one-and-done process—it's an ongoing journey. Once you've laid a strong foundation, the next step is exploring opportunities to expand your knowledge. Professional associations, online resources, mentorships, and networking are all excellent avenues for growth, offering the tools and inspiration to keep your skills sharp and relevant.

Expanding Horizons Through Professional Associations

Engage with Industry Groups

Professional associations like the Association of Proposal Management Professionals (APMP) and the Society for Marketing Professional Services (SMPS) are goldmines for knowledge and connections. These organizations provide more than just networking opportunities—they're a source of cutting-edge insights into industry best practices. By joining, you position yourself to learn from and collaborate with the best in the business.

National and Regional Conferences

Attending conferences hosted by APMP and SMPS can immerse you in the proposal community. From sessions on strategy and content development to workshops on emerging technologies, these events offer actionable insights you can apply immediately. Plus, the interactive nature of panels and Q&A sessions lets you engage directly with industry leaders. When you leave, you'll be armed with new ideas, ready to enhance your next proposal.

Local-Level Participation

While national events are impactful, don't underestimate the value of local chapters. Regional gatherings often offer more personalized and accessible opportunities to learn about market trends and share experiences. These events, whether training sessions, roundtable discussions, or informal networking meetups, are affordable and highly relevant. The connections you make can lead to collaborative partnerships and spark fresh ideas for your work.

Leveraging Online Resources for Continuous Learning

The digital age has made ongoing education more accessible than ever. Online resources offer flexibility and convenience, letting you fit learning into your schedule without skipping a beat.

Stay Updated with Industry Thought Leaders

Follow consultants and industry experts on platforms like LinkedIn, subscribe to newsletters, and engage with online communities. These sources provide a steady stream of insights, trends, and practical tips. For professionals in smaller teams or firms without formal training programs, these resources can be a game changer—delivering actionable knowledge you can apply immediately.

Tap Into E-Learning Platforms

Platforms like YouTube and LinkedIn Learning are treasure troves for professional development. They offer courses tailored to proposal development, including advanced writing techniques, project management, and leadership skills. With the ability to choose content that aligns with your goals, you can focus your learning on areas where you most want to grow.

The Role of Mentorship in Skill Development

Mentorship is a powerful tool for professional growth. Whether you're seeking guidance from an experienced professional or stepping into a mentorship role yourself, the exchange of knowledge is invaluable.

Finding a Mentor

Many organizations, including APMP and SMPS, offer mentorship programs that connect emerging professionals with seasoned veterans. A mentor can provide personalized advice, share lessons learned, and offer a broader perspective on the challenges and opportunities within the field.

Becoming a Mentor

Mentorship isn't just about receiving guidance—it's also about giving back. Serving as a mentor lets you refine your skills as you explain ideas and strategies to others. It's a rewarding experience that fosters professional relationships and strengthens your understanding of the field. Plus, mentoring helps shape the next generation of proposal professionals, contributing to the industry's growth.

Best Practices for Staying at the Forefront

To thrive in proposal development, adopt these best practices:

- **Engage Regularly:** Attend events, participate in discussions, and remain active in professional communities.
- **Stay Curious:** Seek new information through articles, webinars, and courses.
- **Build Relationships:** Leverage your network to foster collaborative learning and exchange ideas.
- **Adapt and Innovate:** Be open to integrating new tools, techniques, and strategies into your workflow.

A Commitment to Lifelong Learning

Proposal development is an ever-evolving field requiring professionals to stay adaptable and proactive. The learning doesn't stop after mastering the basics; it's a lifelong journey. By leveraging professional associations, mentorship, online resources, and local engagement, you can continually grow your skills, remain relevant, and become a valuable asset to your team and organization.

Remember, every step you take in your learning journey enhances your career and your firm's success. Committing to lifelong learning isn't just a personal investment—it's a powerful driver of innovation and growth for the entire industry.

Key Takeaways

- **Leverage Professional Associations:** Join organizations like APMP and SMPS to access events, resources, and networking opportunities that expand your knowledge.

- **Embrace Online Learning:** Use platforms like YouTube and LinkedIn Learning to stay updated on industry trends and sharpen your skills.

- **Pursue Mentorship Opportunities:** Seek a mentor for tailored guidance or become one to refine your skills and give back to the community.

- **Engage Locally:** Attend regional chapter events for cost-effective training and relevant networking opportunities.

- **Commit to Lifelong Learning:** Continuously seek new knowledge and experiences to stay ahead in the dynamic field of proposal development.

NOTES

Chapter 19

Success Stories

Transformative Processes in Action

In proposals, the process behind the scenes can make or break the outcome. Developing a strong, consistent approach to proposal creation isn't just a best practice; it's the cornerstone of success. This chapter explores how a structured process leads to better quality, more efficient workflows, and a more enjoyable experience. Drawing on real-world examples from Kiewit Corporation, James W. Fowler, and Kraemer North America, we'll highlight why disciplined processes are critical and how they can transform your proposal game.

The Role of a Consistent Proposal Process

Think of proposal preparation as planning a road trip. You know your destination, but without a clear map, you risk getting lost, running into detours, and wasting time. A consistent proposal process serves as your roadmap, providing structure and direction while helping you stay on track. Without it, deadlines loom larger, tasks overlap, and chaos creeps in—leading to unnecessary stress and, worse, missed opportunities.

Case Studies: Proven Processes in Action

Kiewit Corporation: Staying the Course Amidst Challenges

Kiewit Corporation faced a daunting task: a high-profile water filtration plant upgrade project in Everett, Washington. Despite having a skilled national proposal team, competing priorities left them short on internal resources. Ideas at Dawn stepped in as a strategic partner, providing what could be described as a navigation system for Kiewit. Ideas at Dawn established a structured proposal management approach early—well before the SOQ was even issued. Weekly status meetings kept the team aligned, ensuring accountability and collaboration throughout the process.

The Outcome

Though Kiewit didn't submit a proposal for the project, their shortlisting during the RFQ phase underscored the power of the process. The experience highlighted how consistency, organization, and teamwork contribute to stronger submissions, even when challenges arise.

James W. Fowler (JWF): Preventing Burnout, Maintaining Momentum

JWF faced a different challenge: multiple strategic pursuits with only one proposal manager to handle them all. This bottleneck threatened team morale and raised the risk of missed deadlines. Ideas at Dawn implemented a streamlined process centered on daily check-ins and clear prioritization. By clearly defining roles and timelines and leading some pursuits, they prevented burnout while maintaining the quality of each submission.

The Outcome

With Ideas at Dawn's structured support, JWF secured shortlists and wins on multiple strategic pursuits. This outcome reflected the effectiveness of a streamlined process and showed how well-managed workloads lead to better results and happier teams.

Kraemer North America: Winning Big Through Structure

Kraemer North America took on a must-win $500 million project for the Colorado Department of Transportation. With limited internal resources, they needed expert guidance to tackle the high stakes and tight timeline. Ideas at Dawn applied its six-step framework, starting six months before the RFP was issued. By focusing on strategic messaging, organizing team schedules, and integrating compelling visuals, they created a seamless, high-quality proposal process.

The Outcome

Kraemer not only made the shortlist but ultimately won the project. The win wasn't just financial—it marked a milestone in Kraemer's growth and reinforced the importance of planning and preparation.

Lessons from Success: Why Process Matters

Consistency as the Backbone of Success

Each example underscores the value of a disciplined, repeatable process. A consistent framework reduces the risk of errors, eliminates last-minute chaos, and lets teams channel their energy into creative storytelling—an essential element of standout proposals.

Engage SMEs Early

SMEs bring critical insights that enrich proposals, from technical expertise to client-centered messaging. Early engagement ensures these contributions are seamlessly integrated, adding depth and differentiation that evaluators notice.

Tailored Support for Every Client

No two pursuits are the same, and successful proposals reflect this. Tailoring your approach—whether focusing on technical graphics, streamlined messaging, or strategic planning—makes sure each submission aligns with the client's unique goals.

Communication Is Key

Clear communication keeps everyone aligned, especially under pressure. Regular check-ins foster collaboration and accountability, creating a proactive environment where potential issues are addressed early. This transparency keeps projects on track and morale high.

The Moral of the Story: Discipline Drives Success

The common thread across these stories? *Success isn't accidental.* It's the result of disciplined processes and collaborative teamwork. Teams that invest in structure and communication increase their chances of winning and foster a more positive experience for everyone involved.

Neglecting structure leads to frustration, wasted resources, and missed opportunities. Focusing on a proven proposal process isn't just about winning the next contract—it's about setting your firm up for sustained success.

The Transformative Power of Process

While no system guarantees a win, a structured approach significantly increases the likelihood of success. A proven process equips teams with the tools they need to navigate the complexities of proposal development, producing submissions that are effective, impactful, and tailored to the client.

By committing to consistency, collaboration, and a client-focused mindset, you can transform your proposals from routine documents into strategic tools that drive results.

Key Takeaways

- **Follow a Proven Framework:** A structured process ensures predictability, reduces errors, and aligns your work with client needs.

- **Engage SMEs Early:** Their technical expertise and insights elevate proposals with customized, client-focused content.

- **Tailor Support to Each Pursuit:** Adapt your approach based on the unique requirements of each client or project.

- **Focus on Communication:** Regular updates, clear expectations, and collaboration keep teams aligned and motivated.

- **Celebrate Collaboration:** Success is a team effort, and every contributor plays an important role in delivering standout proposals.

Chapter 20

Knowledge is Power

Essential Resources for Proposal Development

The phrase "knowledge is power" is particularly relevant for professionals in proposal development. No matter if you're in the AEC industry or another field, maintaining a commitment to learning and growth is essential to staying competitive. The market is always changing, client expectations shift over time, and technology continues to advance. Remaining stagnant is not an option. This chapter will serve as your guide to using resources and strategies that will help you consistently create exceptional and standout proposals.

The Importance of Ongoing Learning

Refining Your Skills

Continuous learning sharpens your technical, strategic, and creative abilities. Like exercising a muscle, the more you practice and expose yourself to fresh ideas, the stronger your skills become. New strategies and techniques equip you with a more robust toolkit to tackle proposal challenges effectively.

Broadening Your Perspective

Ongoing education broadens your horizons, introducing you to innovative ideas from different industries or roles. Think of it like an artist exploring new painting styles—each fresh perspective adds depth and creativity to their work. The same principle applies to proposals; diverse knowledge enhances your ability to create submissions that resonate.

With these benefits in mind, let's explore top resources to support your growth in proposal development.

Top Resources for Proposal Professionals

The Association of Proposal Management Professionals

As a leading organization for proposal professionals, APMP offers many resources tailored to capture management and proposal development.

- **Certifications:** APMP's programs, such as the Foundation and Practitioner certifications, confirm and enhance your skills, giving you a professional edge.
- **Conferences:** Their annual Bid & Proposal Con is a must-attend event. It combines educational sessions with networking opportunities, connecting you with peers and industry leaders who can offer valuable insights and support.

The Society for Marketing Professional Services

For those in the AEC industry, SMPS focuses on aligning marketing and business development with proposal strategies.

- **Workshops and Webinars:** These resources provide actionable strategies for creating proposals that align branding with client needs.

- **Amplify AEC Conference:** This annual event dives into innovative marketing techniques and proposal strategies, equipping you with the tools to make your firm stand out.

Evaluating Training Opportunities

Not all resources are created equally. As you explore learning opportunities, consider these factors:

- **Diverse Perspectives:** Seek resources that offer viewpoints different from your own. For example, technical professionals might benefit from learning creative marketing strategies, while marketers can gain insights into technical writing.

- **Alignment with Goals:** Choose resources that match your specific goals. If your focus is improving visual storytelling, someone like Mike Parkinson is invaluable. For strategic guidance, turn to APMP certifications or tailored workshops.

- **Actionable Takeaways:** Prioritize resources that provide tools or templates you can implement right away, ensuring your learning has a real impact.

The Role of Industry Leaders

Following industry leaders is another way to elevate your knowledge. Their books, workshops, and online content provide a direct line to proven best practices and innovative strategies.

- **Angie Wolfe, Ideas at Dawn:** My workshops focus on refining processes and improving win rates, offering practical strategies to implement immediately.

- **Mike Parkinson, 24 Hour Company:** Known for his expertise in visual storytelling, Mike's techniques help proposal teams create compelling graphics that engage clients and elevate submissions.

- **Baskar Sundaram, Bachuu Scribble:** This resource simplifies proposal development with practical templates and strategies, making complex processes more manageable.

By learning from seasoned professionals, you can integrate tested strategies into your work and enhance your proposals.

Mentorship: A Pathway to Growth

Finding a Mentor

A mentor provides tailored guidance, drawing from their experience to help you navigate challenges and seize opportunities. Organizations like APMP and SMPS often facilitate mentorship programs, connecting emerging professionals with industry veterans.

Becoming a Mentor

Mentorship isn't just for newcomers. By mentoring others, you solidify your knowledge, refine your communication skills, and contribute to the growth of your industry. It's a fulfilling way to give back while continuing to learn and grow.

The Commitment to Lifelong Learning

In proposal development, lifelong learning isn't optional—it's essential. The most successful professionals continuously seek new ideas, tools, and strategies to stay ahead in an evolving marketplace.

By engaging with professional organizations like APMP and SMPS, learning from thought leaders, and fostering mentorship relationships, you create a pathway for continuous improvement. These efforts don't just benefit you—they elevate your entire team and enhance the quality of your proposals.

The takeaway is clear: knowledge is power, and committing to lifelong learning ensures you remain a valuable asset in your field. Equip yourself with the skills and insights to stand out today so you're ready to thrive in the challenges of tomorrow.

Key Takeaways

- **Engage with Professional Organizations:** APMP and SMPS offer certifications, events, and resources tailored to proposal professionals.

- **Leverage Expert Insights:** Follow thought leaders like myself, Mike Parkinson, and Baskar Sundaram for actionable storytelling, design, and process improvement strategies.

- **Seek Diverse Perspectives:** Broaden your horizons by learning from professionals in different roles or industries.

- **Focus on Practical Applications:** Choose training opportunities that provide tools and templates you can implement immediately.

- **Invest in Mentorship:** Build mentor-mentee relationships to foster growth, collaboration, and shared knowledge.

NOTES

Chapter 21

The Key Takeaway

What Every Professional Should Remember

In proposal management, there's a lot riding on getting it right. Tight deadlines, shifting requirements, and the need to stand out in a crowded market can feel overwhelming. So, what's the *secret to success*? It's simpler than you might think: **a consistent process**.

A structured approach doesn't just guide your team; it creates space for innovation and creativity, resulting in strategic and compelling proposals. Let's explore how embracing structure at every stage can transform your proposals—and your team.

The Importance of Kick-Off Meetings: Starting Strong

Imagine starting every proposal with clear direction and alignment. That's the magic of kick-off meetings. These meetings are the foundation of a successful proposal, setting the tone and ensuring everyone is on the same page from day one.

Think of a kick-off meeting as the launchpad for a rocket. Without a solid launch, the entire mission risks failure. During a kick-off meeting, you:

- Define the win themes that will shape your proposal.
- Clarify roles and responsibilities to avoid confusion.
- Outline timelines and milestones to keep the project on track.

When done right, kick-off meetings create a shared purpose, ensuring every team member feels invested in the proposal's success.

SME Involvement: The Secret Ingredient

SMEs are the heart of any successful proposal. Their knowledge elevates your submission from meeting the minimum requirements to speaking to the client's needs. Engaging SMEs early in the process allows you to:

- Gather critical insights that guide the proposal's technical content.
- Customize messaging to address specific client challenges.
- Ensure your proposal stands out as both compliant and compelling.

Think of SMEs as the master chefs in a kitchen. They bring the specialized knowledge and skills that make your proposal resonate with evaluators. Without their input, your proposal risks being bland and generic.

Collaborative Reviews: Refining the Proposal

Drafting the proposal is only half the battle. The real magic happens during the review phase. But let's be clear: reviews shouldn't feel like disconnected edits and comments. Instead, they should function like a team huddle—a chance to strategize and refine together. Collaborative reviews provide opportunities to:

- Refine messaging to align with client priorities and win themes.
- Ensure compliance with all RFx requirements.
- Foster accountability among team members, creating a shared sense of ownership.

By treating reviews as a team effort, you elevate the quality of the proposal, creating a final product that is polished, cohesive, and impactful.

The Benefits of a Consistent Process

So why invest in structure? Because a consistent process does more than improve proposals—it transforms how your team operates. Benefits of a structured approach include:

- **Reduced Stress:** Clear roles and timelines eliminate last-minute scrambling.
- **Stronger Team Dynamics:** A supportive and collaborative environment boosts morale.
- **Higher Win Rates:** Proposals that resonate with clients are more likely to succeed.

Driving Results Through Teamwork

When teams embrace a structured process, they achieve more than just compliance—they create winning submissions. It's like planting a well-tended garden: prepare the soil, plant carefully, and you'll reap the rewards.

With clear communication, shared goals, and a focus on quality, teams are more efficient, creative, and productive. The result? Proposals that meet requirements and leave a lasting impression on clients.

Leadership's Role in Reinforcing the Process

As the proposal manager and leader, your role is critical in embedding a consistent proposal process into your organization's culture. Here's how you can make it stick:

- **Provide Training:** Teach your team the value of kick-off meetings, SME involvement, and collaborative reviews.

- **Document the Process:** Create easy-to-follow guides or checklists that outline the steps for a successful proposal.
- **Model Best Practices:** Lead by example, showing how structure and collaboration result in better outcomes.

By reinforcing these principles, you're improving proposals and building a culture of excellence.

The Cost of Ignoring Structure

Still skeptical?

Consider the alternative. Teams without a consistent process often experience the following:

- Missed deadlines and rushed submissions.
- Errors that slip through due to poor coordination.
- Burnout and frustration among team members.

On the other hand, organizations that focus on structure are more **resilient**, **adaptable**, and **successful**—even under pressure.

Winning proposals don't happen by accident. They're the result of thoughtful planning, collaboration, and execution.

Collaboration + Structure = Success

The key to proposal success lies in collaboration and structure. By starting with strategic kick-off meetings, engaging SMEs early, and fostering collaborative reviews, you create a process that ensures quality and predictability.

Every winning proposal is a team effort—a blend of structure, creativity, and shared commitment. With a consistent process, you'll meet and exceed client expectations, setting your firm apart in a competitive market.

The Final Lesson: Build for Success

Proposals aren't just about meeting deadlines—they're about creating opportunities. By embracing structure and collaboration, you're laying the foundation for long-term success. Take what you've learned here, implement it with intention, and watch your proposals evolve into powerful tools that drive results.

> ### Key Takeaways
>
> - **Emphasize Kick-Off Meetings:** Launch every proposal with clear goals, roles, and timelines to set the stage for success.
>
> - **Involve SMEs Early:** Collaborate with experts to craft technical, accurate, and client-focused messaging.
>
> - **Make Reviews Collaborative:** Use team discussions to refine and align content for maximum impact.
>
> - **Foster a Consistent Process:** Develop a repeatable framework that brings structure and efficiency to every pursuit.
>
> - **Communicate the Value of Collaboration:** Reinforce the importance of these practices through training, documentation, and leading by example.

NOTES

Chapter 22

Getting Started

Implementing Strategies for Immediate Impact

Managing proposals can sometimes feel like an endless juggling act—tight deadlines, shifting priorities, and the constant pressure to win new business. It's easy to get caught in the cycle of reactive work, leaving little space for strategic planning or process improvement. But here's the good news: transforming your approach doesn't have to be overwhelming. By focusing on manageable, high-impact changes, you can create a foundation for long-term success while streamlining your workflow.

Start with a Kick-Off Meeting

The first step in transforming your proposal process is straightforward yet powerful: *hold a kick-off meeting*. This isn't just a check-the-box activity; it's the cornerstone of a successful proposal. Think of it as the team's huddle before the big game—it's where everyone gets aligned and energized for what's ahead.

In your kick-off meeting, cover these three essential elements:

- **Define the Win Themes:** Clarify what the client values and ensure these themes drive the proposal narrative.

- **Assign Roles and Responsibilities:** Every team member should know exactly what they're responsible for, from research to writing to review.

- **Set Timelines and Deadlines:** Establish a realistic schedule to keep everyone on track and accountable.

By laying this groundwork, you'll foster teamwork, eliminate confusion, and create a shared sense of purpose—all critical ingredients for success.

Incorporate Collaborative Review Meetings

If your team is already conducting kick-off meetings, the next opportunity for improvement lies in your review process. Instead of relying on isolated reviewers or passing drafts back and forth, bring the team together for collaborative review meetings.

These sessions go beyond surface-level edits, encouraging deeper conversations about strategy, messaging, and compliance. To make them effective:

- **Focus on Key Sections:** Instead of tackling the entire document at once, concentrate on one or two sections to avoid feeling overwhelmed.

- **Assign a Facilitator:** Typically, the proposal manager, the facilitator, ensures the discussion stays on track and that all voices are heard.

- **Encourage Team Investment:** Collaborative reviews make team members feel more connected to the proposal, which boosts their commitment to its success.

By combining diverse perspectives, you'll refine the proposal's messaging and elevate its overall quality, creating a product that truly reflects the expertise of your entire team.

Integrate Technology and AI Tools

For teams with a solid foundation, integrating technology can be a game changer, amplifying efficiency and enhancing outcomes. Consider incorporating tools that streamline workflows and reduce manual effort:

- **CRM Systems:** Centralize client and project information for easy access and streamlined collaboration.

- **Content Databases:** Organize past proposals, resumes, and project details to save time and ensure consistency.

- **AI Writing Tools:** Applications like ChatGPT or Perplexity can draft content, perform preliminary research, and tailor messaging to client needs.

Imagine having an AI draft the first 80% of your proposal, letting your team focus on refinement, strategy, and storytelling. These tools don't replace creativity and expertise—they enhance them, giving you time to focus on the elements that make your proposal shine.

Measuring the Impact of Changes

Once you've implemented these strategies, how do you know they're working? Measuring impact is critical for continuous improvement. Track key metrics like:

- **Efficiency:** How long does it take to complete the different steps of the process?

- **Quality:** Are compliance errors going down? Is the content more aligned with client expectations?

- **Win Rates:** Have you won more proposals since making these changes?

In addition, conduct post-submission debriefs with your team to gather qualitative feedback on what worked and what didn't. Tools like Clockify can help track productivity and pinpoint areas for further refinement. Over time, these evaluations will highlight trends and opportunities, helping you continuously optimize your process.

The Roadmap to Long-Term Success

New strategies aren't a one-time effort—it's an iterative journey. As your team adapts to changes, regular reviews of your workflows will let you incorporate lessons learned and experiment with new tools or approaches.

The benefits of this commitment to growth are transformative. Over time, you'll see:

- Reduced stress levels as workflows become more predictable.

- Higher team morale driven by clear processes and collaborative efforts.

Proposals that resonate more effectively with clients, leading to higher win rates. This feedback loop—powered by metrics, reviews, and collaboration—creates an environment of continuous improvement and shared success.

Small Changes, Big Impact

The key to elevating your proposal management process isn't about overhauling everything overnight. Real transformation comes from small, deliberate changes that build on one another. By focusing on foundational elements like kick-off meetings, collaborative reviews, and technology integration, you'll create a ripple effect that improves efficiency, quality, and outcomes.

Remember, every journey begins with a single step. Whether you're scheduling your first kick-off meeting, rethinking your review strategy, or exploring new tech tools, the changes you make today will pave the way for success. Consistency and intention are your most powerful allies, turning incremental improvements into game-changing results.

Key Takeaways

- **Start with Kick-Off Meetings:** Align your team from the start by setting clear goals, roles, and deadlines.

- **Make Reviews Collaborative:** Turn reviews into team discussions to refine content and ensure compliance.

- **Leverage Technology:** Use tools like AI, CRMs, and content databases to streamline workflows and focus on strategy.

- **Track Your Progress:** Measure efficiency, quality, and win rates to evaluate the impact of new approaches.

- **Focus on Incremental Changes:** Small, consistent improvements can lead to big, transformative results.

NOTES

Chapter 23

The One Change

Focusing on a Single Improvement in Proposal Approach

Proposal development often feels like a race against the clock. Deadlines loom, priorities shift, and the pressure to deliver can be intense. In the scramble to submit, many teams default to working in isolation, focusing on speed over quality. But here's the truth: solo efforts often lead to proposals riddled with errors, overlooked opportunities, and messaging that misses the mark with clients. If one strategy can transform your proposal process, it's this: adopt structured reviews.

Why Structured Reviews Are Essential

Think of structured reviews as your secret weapon. They bring multiple perspectives into the process, enhancing the quality of your submission in ways a single author could never achieve.

Imagine preparing for an important presentation. *Would you wing it without seeking feedback?* Probably not. The same principle applies to proposals. A well-executed review process leverages your team's collective expertise, resulting in a document that's polished, accurate, and tailored to the client's needs.

The benefits of team input include:

- **Technical Precision:** SMEs ensure accuracy in technical details.

- **Strategic Clarity:** Leaders refine win themes and align the proposal with client priorities.

- **Polished Messaging:** Writers ensure the proposal is cohesive, persuasive, and compliant.

When you tap into the diverse strengths of your team, your proposal becomes more than a document—it becomes a strategic tool that resonates with clients.

Spotting Errors Before They Become Costly

One of the greatest advantages of a structured review is catching mistakes before they derail your submission. Typos, inconsistencies, or compliance gaps can be easy to miss when you're deep in the weeds.

Think of a review as a fresh set of eyes. Reviewers can spot the issues the original author might overlook. In proposal development, where a single error can disqualify your submission, these reviews are not just helpful—they're essential.

The stakes:

- **Typos and Formatting Errors:** While seemingly minor, they can make your proposal seem rushed or unprofessional.

- **Compliance Oversights:** Missing a requirement could mean automatic disqualification.

- **Misaligned Messaging:** Failing to address the client's priorities weakens your proposal's impact.

With a structured review process, you safeguard your proposal against these risks, ensuring your submission is both polished and compliant.

Enhancing Client Focus

Structured reviews also sharpen your client focus. Collaborative discussions during reviews ensure your win themes and messaging align with the client's top priorities.

Clients don't just want solutions—they want to feel understood. A team that collaborates effectively on reviews can better articulate how their proposal addresses the client's unique needs.

The Result: A proposal that doesn't just check boxes but tells a compelling story about why your firm is the right choice.

How Structured Reviews Transform Proposals

Incorporating structured reviews into your process creates proposals that stand out.

- **Feedback Fine-Tunes Content:** Constructive input ensures your messaging is clear, concise, and compelling.
- **Stronger Team Alignment:** Reviews foster a sense of shared ownership, encouraging accountability and pride.
- **A Polished Final Product:** Collaborative efforts produce a cohesive, high-quality proposal reflecting your team's best work.

Overcoming Barriers to Structured Reviews

While the benefits are clear, implementing structured reviews can feel challenging. Here's how to address common hurdles:

1. Time Constraints

Tight deadlines often lead teams to skip reviews, but these short-term "savings" can cost you in the long run.

Solution: Schedule reviews as milestones from the outset. Build them into your timeline as non-negotiable steps.

2. Resistance to Change

Some team members may be hesitant to adopt new processes, preferring to stick to familiar workflows.

Solution: Highlight the benefits of reviews, such as fewer errors and stronger alignment with client priorities. Share success stories from previous proposals to illustrate their value.

3. Lack of Structure

Unstructured reviews can devolve into chaotic discussions with little productive output.

Solution: Assign roles for each meeting, a facilitator to guide the discussion, and a note-taker to document actionable feedback. Focus each review session on specific parts — messaging, and visuals—to keep conversations productive.

Starting Small: Introducing Reviews

If your team is new to structured reviews, start small to build comfort and familiarity:

- **Schedule a Single Review Meeting:** Choose one section, like the executive summary, as the focus of your first session.

- **Assign Roles:** Designate a facilitator, usually the proposal manager, to lead the discussion and a note-taker to document feedback.

- **Foster Constructive Feedback:** Encourage actionable suggestions over vague critiques. For example, replace "This section is unclear" with "Can we rephrase this section to highlight how we'll achieve the client's goals?"

These small steps ensure your reviews are manageable and productive from the start.

Measuring the Impact

To understand the effectiveness of structured reviews, track key metrics over time:

- **Reduction in Errors:** Are typos, compliance gaps, or inconsistencies less frequent?

- **Engagement Levels:** Are team members participating actively in discussions?

- **Win Rates:** Are your proposals seeing higher success rates after adopting structured reviews?

Regularly assessing these factors will help refine your process and highlight its value to the team.

The Game Changer for Proposal Success

If there's one change to focus on in your proposal process, make it structured reviews. The insights and collaboration gained during reviews don't just reduce errors—they elevate your proposals into compelling, client-focused submissions.

Why It Matters: Collaboration isn't a luxury; it's a necessity. Structured reviews ensure your proposals aren't just compliant but resonate deeply with the client's needs.

Key Takeaways

- **Leverage Team Collaboration:** Multiple perspectives during reviews result in stronger, more polished proposals.

- **Address Common Barriers:** Overcome time constraints and resistance by scheduling reviews early and highlighting their benefits.

- **Start Small:** Begin with one review meeting focused on a single section to ease your team into the process.

- **Track Results:** Measure the impact of reviews through error reduction, team engagement, and improved win rates.

- **Commit to the Process:** Treat reviews as an important part of proposal success, not an optional step.

NOTES

Chapter 24

The Future Landscape

Evolving Proposal Development in AEC

The proposal industry is on the cusp of transformative changes in how proposals are crafted. As technology evolves and client expectations shift, the future of proposal development promises to be more efficient, data-driven, and collaborative. Whether you're a proposal coordinator, manager, or a seller-doer, staying ahead of these trends is essential to thrive in this dynamic landscape.

AI and Automation: Revolutionizing Efficiency

Imagine an assistant who drafts proposal content, researches background information, and tailors messaging specifically to your client's needs. That's the power of artificial intelligence.

Tools like ChatGPT and other advanced AI platforms are poised to reshape the proposal development process in the AEC industry.

AI doesn't just draft content—it transforms workflows. Automated compliance checks, document organization, and data analysis save valuable time. Think of automation as a personal assistant handling routine tasks, freeing you to focus on strategy and creativity. *The result?* Proposals that are not just faster to produce but also sharper and more impactful.

Enhanced Collaboration with Advanced Technology

In today's hybrid and remote work environments, collaboration isn't just nice to have—it's essential. Imagine trying to prepare a multi-course meal with your team, but each person is working in a separate kitchen. The lack of connection leads to inefficiencies and missed opportunities.

Integrated platforms like Asana, Microsoft Teams, and Slack are evolving to meet the specific needs of proposal teams. These tools enable real-time communication, centralized resource sharing, and collaborative editing. It's like bringing your team into a single kitchen where everyone works together seamlessly, creating a cohesive and efficient proposal process.

Data-Driven Insights for Tailored Proposals

In today's information-rich world, data is your secret weapon. Think of your firm's past projects and client interactions as a goldmine of insights. Using CRM tools and advanced analytics, proposal teams can uncover patterns in client preferences, winning strategies, and industry trends.

A well-maintained CRM can guide your approach, helping you identify what resonates with specific clients. It's like a coach studying game footage to refine a winning strategy. By leveraging these insights, you can craft personalized, client-focused proposals that outshine generic, one-size-fits-all submissions.

Sustainability and Social Responsibility

Clients are increasingly focusing on sustainability and social responsibility in their decision-making processes. Proposals must now reflect a firm's commitment to these values.

This could mean showcasing your green building practices, highlighting diverse and inclusive project teams, or emphasizing community impact. Just as consumers gravitate toward brands that align with their values, clients are drawn to firms that focus on sustainability and inclusion. By weaving these priorities into your proposals, you stand out and build stronger, trust-based relationships.

Preparing for the Future

To stay competitive in this evolving landscape, proposal professionals must take proactive steps to prepare:

- **Embrace Technology:** Familiarize yourself with AI tools and collaboration platforms. Think of these as essential tools in your toolbox—the more you understand, the more effectively you can use them to build standout proposals.

- **Stay Agile:** Be ready to adapt to emerging trends while holding on to strategies that work. Like an athlete constantly refining their performance, flexibility is key to staying ahead.

- **Invest in Training:** Professional development through workshops, webinars, and certifications—such as those offered by APMP and SMPS—keeps your skills sharp and relevant.

- **Foster Collaboration:** Create opportunities for internal teamwork to flourish. Collaboration isn't just beneficial in the proposal world—it's critical to creating well-rounded, compelling submissions.

The Benefits of Embracing Change

The rewards for adapting to these trends are clear:

- **Increased Efficiency:** Automation frees up time for strategic thinking and creativity.

- **Improved Win Rates:** Personalized, data-informed proposals resonate more effectively with clients.

- **Stronger Team Dynamics:** Advanced collaboration tools enhance teamwork and engagement, creating a supportive and unified workforce.

Thriving in a Changing Industry

Proposal development in the AEC industry is at a tipping point. By leveraging technology, fostering collaboration, and aligning with client values like sustainability, you can stay ahead of the curve and position your firm as a leader in the market.

The key takeaway?

Collaboration and strategy are at the heart of every winning proposal. Structured reviews, advanced technology, and data-driven insights create a foundation for proposals that don't just meet requirements—they tell a story that resonates deeply with clients.

Now is the time to embrace these changes, refine your processes, and set your firm up for long-term success in an increasingly competitive landscape.

Key Takeaways

- **Adopt AI and Automation:** Streamline workflows and boost efficiency with cutting-edge tools.

- **Leverage Data for Personalization:** Use CRM and analytics to craft client-focused submissions.

- **Invest in Collaboration Tools:** Seamless teamwork is essential for creating cohesive, high-quality proposals.

- **Focus on Sustainability:** Align with client values to stand out in a competitive market.

- **Stay Agile and Proactive:** Continuous learning and adaptability will position you to excel in an ever-changing industry.

NOTES

Chapter 25

Navigating Overwhelm

Final Advice for Proposal Professionals

The pressure to meet tight deadlines while managing multiple priorities can be unrelenting. Imagine this: it's peak proposal season, your inbox is overflowing, and you're trying to figure out which urgent task to tackle first. It can feel overwhelming, even paralyzing. However, the good news is that it doesn't have to be this way.

Overwhelm often boils down to two main culprits: lack of structure and an all-or-nothing mindset. Without a clear approach, tasks pile up, leading to chaos and late nights. Combine this with the pursuit of perfection or a win-at-all-costs mentality, and you've got a recipe for burnout. Recognizing these pitfalls is the first step to reclaiming control and transforming the proposal process into something manageable and even rewarding.

Shifting Your Mindset: From Chaos to Clarity

The most powerful tool to combat overwhelm isn't software or processes—it's a mindset shift. Instead of viewing the proposal process as a giant, insurmountable task, reframe it as a sequence of achievable steps. Think of it like building a puzzle—one piece at a time.

Focus on progress, not perfection. No proposal is flawless, and that's okay. Your goal should be to deliver a strong, client-focused document that checks all the boxes—not an unattainable masterpiece. Allow yourself and your team to celebrate progress at each stage. By shifting your mindset to embrace progress, you'll create a healthier, more productive work environment.

The Power of Collaboration

Don't forget: you're not in this alone. Proposal development is a team effort, and leaning into collaboration can lighten the load while elevating the end product.

- **Kick-Off Meeting and Check-Ins:** Start with a well-organized kick-off meeting to align on goals, assign roles, and clarify deadlines. Regular check-ins help maintain momentum and ensure accountability.

- **Collaborative Reviews:** Bring your team together for structured review sessions. These aren't just about catching errors—they're about blending perspectives and strengthening the proposal's overall message.

Collaboration fosters creativity, making sure your proposal reflects a range of ideas and insights that a solo effort can't achieve.

Celebrate the Small Wins

In the whirlwind of deadlines, it's easy to overlook the importance of celebrating progress. But taking a moment to acknowledge achievements—no matter how small—can make a big difference in morale.

Have you finished an outline? That's a win.

Did you get positive feedback from a review session? Another win.

Recognizing these milestones maintains momentum and motivates the team to keep pushing forward. Proposal development is a marathon, not a sprint, and celebrating along the way can sustain energy and focus.

Quick Wins to Regain Control

When you're drowning in tasks, small changes can create immediate relief.

- **Start with an Organized Kick-Off Meeting:** Align on goals, assign responsibilities, and set deadlines. Starting with clarity eliminates confusion and reduces stress later.

- **Break It Down:** Focus on one section or task at a time instead of being overwhelmed by the whole document.

- **Use Task Management Tools:** Platforms like Microsoft Teams, Trello, or Asana help you track progress and stay organized.

Integrating Technology

Technology is a game changer when managing overwhelm.

- **Automation Tools:** Use Grammarly or PerfectIt to handle grammar checks and compliance.

- **AI Writing Assistants:** Tools like ChatGPT and Perplexity can generate drafts or help tailor messaging, saving time for higher-level strategy.

By automating repetitive tasks, you'll free up energy to focus on refining content and sharpening your proposal's narrative.

Overcoming Barriers to Change

Even the best strategies can encounter resistance. Here's how to tackle common challenges:

- **Collaboration Resistance:** Some team members may see collaboration as more work. Emphasize benefits like shared accountability and improved outcomes, and lead by example to show its value.

- **Fear of Delegation:** it is hard to let go, but trusting your team is critical. Start by delegating smaller tasks like formatting or compliance reviews to build confidence in your team's capabilities.

Time Constraints: Investing in Efficiency

You might think you don't have time for meetings or structured reviews, but investing time upfront can save you hours later. A strong kick-off meeting or well-organized review process prevents rework and makes sure everyone is aligned from the start.

Building Resilience for Future Proposals

While addressing short-term overwhelm is essential, building resilience is the key to long-term success.

- **Create Reusable Templates:** Streamline future proposals by developing templates for common sections like resumes, project descriptions, and cover letters.
- **Establish Clear Workflows:** Document your processes to ensure consistency and make onboarding new team members easier.
- **Invest in Training:** Workshops, webinars, and industry conferences can keep you up-to-date on best practices and new tools.

Turning Stress into Success

Proposal overwhelm doesn't have to define your process. By shifting your mindset, focusing on collaboration, and breaking tasks into manageable pieces, you can turn stress into success.

Keep it simple:

- Lean on your team for support.
- Celebrate progress, not perfection.
- Embrace tools and workflows that streamline the process.

Every small change you make today is a step toward a more efficient, less stressful future. You've got this—one task, one milestone, one proposal at a time.

Key Takeaways

- **Focus on Progress, Not Perfection:** Celebrate incremental achievements to maintain momentum and reduce stress.

- **Start with a Kick-Off Meeting:** Set clear expectations, align your team, and define roles from the outset.

- **Break Tasks Into Manageable Pieces:** Approach the proposal step-by-step instead of tackling it all at once.

- **Leverage Technology:** Automate repetitive tasks with tools like Grammarly and AI writing assistants.

NOTES

Chapter 26

Conclusion

Congratulations! Your journey from chaos to clarity begins. You've reached the end of *From Chaos to Clarity*, and now you're equipped with transformative strategies to redefine how you approach proposal development. Let's reflect and plan how to bring these ideas to life—boosting your win rates and reducing the stress that often goes along with proposal work.

Why Structure Matters

At the core of successful proposal development lies a consistent, structured process. Why is this so important? Because clarity creates confidence. A repeatable framework, with foundational steps like structured kick-off meetings and collaborative reviews, sets your team up for success. A structured process:

- **Defines Roles**: Everyone knows their responsibilities, so nothing slips through the cracks.

- **Sets Clear Expectations:** Deadlines, objectives, and priorities are well understood, reducing confusion.

- **Lowers Stress:** With everyone aligned, you can focus on strategy and quality instead of last-minute chaos.

When you bring order to your approach, your team moves from scrambling to purposefully crafting proposals that reflect their best work.

Collaboration Is Non-Negotiable

Here's a truth that bears repeating: ***no one person can create a winning proposal alone***. The magic happens when you leverage the skills and insights of your SMEs, designers, and team members. Involve them early, keep communication open, and foster a sense of shared ownership. Collaboration doesn't just enhance proposal quality—it transforms the experience. Teams that work together feel more connected, supported, and inspired. And that camaraderie translates into thoughtful, polished, and client-centered proposals.

Customize for Impact

One size does not fit all when it comes to proposals. Clients want to feel understood, and that means tailoring every part of your submission to their unique challenges and priorities. Avoid generic, boilerplate content at all costs. Instead:

- **Tailor Your Narrative:** Use language that speaks directly to the client's needs and aspirations.

- **Personalize Visuals:** Integrate graphics and images that emphasize your alignment with their goals.

- **Focus Your Messaging:** Highlight how your solutions solve their specific problems, showing your attentiveness and expertise.

By showing clients, "We hear you, and we have the solutions you need," you position your team as a true partner—not just a bidder.

Technology: Your Best Ally

Today, technology is no longer a luxury—it's a necessity. CRM systems, content databases, and AI-driven writing assistants can revolutionize your workflow. Here's how technology can help:

- **Streamline Workflows:** Centralize client information and access past project data with CRMs.

- **Automate Repetitive Tasks:** Use tools like Grammarly or PerfectIt for editing, freeing up time for strategy.

- **Enhance Creativity:** Leverage AI writing tools to draft content so your team can focus on refining and storytelling.

Technology isn't here to replace your knowledge but to amplify it. With the right tools, you can work smarter, not harder.

Commit to Continuous Improvement

The proposal journey doesn't end with submission. Debriefs, metrics, and industry trends are your allies in the pursuit of continuous improvement. After every proposal:

- **Debrief as a Team:** What worked? What didn't? Use feedback to refine your process.

- **Track Metrics:** Monitor win rates and compliance issues and review feedback to identify areas for growth.

- **Stay Current:** Attend workshops, read industry updates, and embrace new tools to stay ahead of the curve.

This commitment to learning transforms setbacks into opportunities, making sure your next proposal is always better than the last.

The Client Is the Hero

Every winning proposal has one thing in common: it puts the client at the center. Shift the focus away from showcasing your firm's capabilities and emphasize how you will help clients meet their goals. Every section of your proposal—narrative, visuals, and technical details—should reinforce this central idea:

- We understand you.
- We're aligned with your priorities.
- We'll deliver results that matter.

This client-focused approach builds trust and creates a foundation for long-term partnerships.

Tackling Overwhelm

Finally, let's talk about the elephant in the room: proposal overwhelm. Deadlines can make the process feel daunting, but with the right mindset and strategies, you can transform stress into success. Here's how:

- **Break It Down:** Focus on manageable steps instead of the entire proposal at once.
- **Celebrate Small Wins:** Every milestone—no matter how small—is progress worth acknowledging.
- **Build Team Support:** Lean on your team to share the load and bring diverse perspectives to the table.

With these practices, even the most complex proposal becomes a manageable and rewarding challenge.

The Journey Ahead

As you step forward, take these actionable insights and make them your own. Define your structured process, foster collaboration, tailor your messaging, and embrace the power of technology. Your journey *from chaos to clarity* is beginning, and the steps you take today will lead to more compelling, client-focused proposals tomorrow. Winning proposals aren't accidents—they're the result of intentional, thoughtful, and strategic efforts. You have the tools, the knowledge, and the mindset to succeed. Now, it's time to put them into action. The future of proposal excellence starts with you. You've got this. Let's create winning proposals—one thoughtful step at a time.

About The Author

Angie Wolfe

When proposal development often feels overwhelming and chaotic, Angie Wolfe, CP APMP, has delivered a game-changing resource. Her book, "*From Chaos to Clarity: Unlock the Proven Process to Boost Your Win Rates*," is a must-read for professionals looking to bring structure, efficiency, and success to their proposal efforts.

Angie wrote this book with a clear purpose: to empower professionals who manage proposal development. She knows firsthand the challenges they face—tight deadlines, the need to create compelling content, and the ever-present pressure to stand out in a competitive marketplace. With "*From Chaos to Clarity,*" Angie equips readers with actionable strategies to turn these challenges into opportunities, enabling them to craft client-focused proposals that win.

Meet Angie Wolfe, Your Guide to Proposal Success

With over 20 years of experience in business development and marketing for Fortune 500 companies, Angie brings a lot of knowledge to the table. She founded Ideas at Dawn Marketing Consultants in 2019, a woman-owned business dedicated to helping civil engineering and construction firms secure more work—without adding to their payroll burden. Angie has built her reputation as a trusted expert by managing billion-dollar pursuits and sharing her insights as a sought-after speaker at AEC industry conferences and webinars.

Her mission is simple yet powerful: *to help proposal professionals work smarter, not harder, and achieve the success they've always envisioned.*

Why Read "From Chaos to Clarity"?

This isn't just another book about proposal writing—it's a comprehensive guide that transforms your approach. Angie provides a proven framework designed to:

- Simplify the proposal process.
- Increase efficiency.
- Help you craft submissions that resonate with clients.

Whether you're new to proposal management or a seasoned pro, this book will help you streamline your workflows, reduce stress, and boost your win rates.

Ready to Transform Your Proposals?

Don't wait to make the changes that will elevate your proposals from average to exceptional. Dive into "From Chaos to Clarity" today and discover the tools and strategies you need to:

- Streamline your process.
- Create compelling, client-focused proposals.
- Win more work—and with less stress.

Join Angie's growing community on LinkedIn for ongoing support, insights, and inspiration as you take your proposal development skills to the next level.

The journey *from chaos to clarity* starts now—are you ready to win?

Unlock Proposal Success

Transform Chaos into Clarity!

*A*re you a professional tangled in the chaotic web of proposal development? Do **last-minute scrambles** and **overwhelming processes** haunt you at each submission? It's time to take control of your proposal game!

Introducing our game-changing **Proposal Training Series**, designed for professionals like you who dream of producing *compelling, client-focused proposals* with **less stress** and **greater efficiency**.

Here's What You'll Discover:

1. The AEC Proposal System™

Streamline your proposal process by mastering a foolproof system that gives clarity to every stage of development.

2. Unlock the Power of Tools and AI in Proposal Development

Leverage cutting-edge technologies that make your proposals not just easier but smarter.

3. Six Proven Ways to Get Content from Your SMEs

Transform the way you gather input from SMEs, ensuring you capture invaluable insights without chasing them down.

4. Mastering the Art of Storyboarding

Craft proposals that not only inform but ignite interest. Learn to storyboard your submissions for an impactful narrative that speaks directly to your clients.

5. Five Practices to Improve Your Leadership

Empower your proposal team with essential leadership skills to foster collaboration and accountability, turning individual strengths into unified success.

Why Choose Our Trainings?

- **Empowered Transformation:** Our training equips you with proven strategies and actionable techniques that turn overwhelm into clarity. Say goodbye to the chaotic submission process and hello to winning proposals!

- **Collaboration and Team Alignment:** Break down silos! Our structured processes improve communication and responsibility, ensuring everyone on your team is working toward the same goal.

Imagine submitting proposals that are cohesive, polished, and strategically aligned. Imagine working smarter, not harder, while watching your measurable results soar!

Ready to Elevate Your Proposal Success?

Don't let chaotic processes hold you back. It's time to step into a world where clarity reigns.

Visit https://keap.app/booking/ideasatdawn/from-chaos-to-clarity or scan the QR code below to discuss your specific needs and find the perfect training for your team!

For personalized guidance on which training will best help you reach your goals, visit our website, or contact us directly.

Transform your approach, elevate your submissions, and unlock proposal success today!

Your clients are waiting.

www.ingramcontent.com/pod-product-compliance
Lightning Source LLC
Chambersburg PA
CBHW050518100526
44581CB00001B/19